Revised Edition

Jesus & You

Discovering The
Real Christ

MICHAEL PENNOCK

Ave Maria Press   Notre Dame, Indiana

Permissions:

Excerpts from *The Jerusalem Bible,* copyright © 1966, 1967 and 1968 by Darton, Longman & Todd, Ltd. and Doubleday & Company, Inc. are used by permission of the publishers.

Excerpts from *The Documents of Vatican II* are reprinted with permission of America Press, Inc., 106 West 56 Street, New York, NY 10019. © 1966. All rights reserved.

Nihil Obstat:
   Rev. Mark A. DiNardo
   Censor Deputatus
Imprimatur:
   Most Rev. James A. Hickey, S.T.D.
   Bishop of Cleveland

© 1984 Ave Maria Press, Notre Dame, Indiana 46556

Library of Congress Catalog Card Number: 84-70384

International Standard Book Number: 0-87793-315-4

Photography:
   Paul Buddle, 86; Ed Carlin, 20; Alan Cliburn, 79; Vivienne della Grotta, 220; John E. Fitzgerald, 38, 50, 66; The Genesis Project, Inc., 60, 92, 118, 139, 177; Israeli Tourist Bureau, 12; Jean-Claude Lejeune, 6; Panographics, 37, 151, 212; Gene Plaisted, 75, 134, 170, 204; Religious News Service, 25, 27, 112, 128, 156, 190, 195, 217; Paul M. Schrock, 107; Bob Taylor, 34, 164.

Manufactured in the United States of America.

DEDICATION

This book is dedicated to Father Paul Hritz, Ph.D.,
pastor of St. Malachi Church in Cleveland, Ohio.
He is a teacher *par excellence*
whose theological vision has greatly formed me.
He is a friend who makes Jesus
real by the way he lives.
For his friendship, for his encouragement,
for his inspiration, I thank him.

Acknowledgments

Once again I would like to thank here those individuals who helped with the first edition of this book. Special thanks to Jim Finley, an outstanding religious educator and friend, who co-authored with me the first edition of *Jesus and You*. The love of our wives, Kaye Finley and Carol Pennock, supported and sustained us in our initial writing projects. They have been a sign of our Lord's love to us.

Sincere thanks to the following individuals: Father Joe McHugh, S.J., lent his considerable editorial skills. Sister Mary Charles Ann, S.N.D., contributed some practical hints. Our original editor, Gene Geissler of Ave Maria Press, along with Charlie Jones of Ave, gave us much support and encouragement. My present editors, Frank Cunningham and Joan Bellina, have given me outstanding assistance in producing this edition of the book.

The following people deserve thanks for their insights and comments: Father Don Cozzens, Ph.D., Sister Cathy Hilkert, O.P., Sister Pat Kozak, C.S.J., Sister Hope Greener, C.S.J., Lora Robbins, Sister Mary Owen, S.N.D., Sister Dorothy Sarrachen, O.P., Jim and Judy Brogan, Al and Sandy Musca, Blair and Barb Chirdon, Dale Gabor, Sharon Chester, Bill Todia, Martha Oakes, Maryanne Myers and former students Matt McDonnell, Bill Marquardt, Mike Comella, Dave Cinolotac, Steve Spittler and Neal Stovicek. Former Director of Religious Education for the Cleveland Diocese, Father Mark DiNardo, Ph.D., a friend and mentor, has been a continual source of inspiration.

Special thanks go to the students of St. Ignatius High School, Cleveland, for their continued positive response to this book. Joe Popelka and Joe Pophal both offered their helpful insights and suggestions for this updated edition. They typify the outstanding young people I have been privileged to share the good news with over the years.

Finally, much gratitude to Dan Gaugler for his valuable assistance on this new edition. This remarkable young man typifies the joy that can be found in the gospel of Jesus Christ.

Contents

INTRODUCTION:
Jesus and You

All history is incomprehensible without Christ.
—Ernest Renan

The strange thing about Jesus is that you can never get away from him.
—a Japanese student

As you open the pages of this book, you are beginning a journey—a journey which has as its outcome a better knowledge of Jesus Christ.

What do *you* think of Jesus Christ?

This is the most important question that can possibly be asked of you. Jesus himself asks it. In perhaps the most famous passage of Mark's gospel, Jesus poses this very question:

> "Who do people say I am?" And they told him. "John the Baptist," they said "others Elijah; others again, one of the prophets." "But you," he asked "who do you say I am?" Peter spoke up and said to him, "You are the Christ" (Mk 8:27-29).

Many intelligent and good men and women down through the centuries have believed that Jesus is the Messiah (the Christ), the Son of the Living God, who has achieved salvation from sin and victory over death for all people. Jesus has made all the difference in their lives.

What difference does Jesus make in your life? What kind of companion is he on your life journey? Is he the silent partner who is always there to help you, to take care of your needs in both good and bad times? Where do you stand with Jesus?

Before beginning your study of Jesus, pause here and honestly reflect on who Jesus is for you. The following attitude survey will help you search your heart for answers to the questions posed above.

7

MY BELIEFS ABOUT JESUS

Mark the following statements according to this code:

SA — Strongly agree; I firmly believe this

A — Agree; I believe this

DK — Don't know; I honestly don't know what I believe about this

D — Disagree; I don't believe this

_____ 1. Jesus is the Messiah (the Christ), Son of the Living God.

_____ 2. Jesus is the way to freedom.

_____ 3. Jesus is my personal savior.

_____ 4. Jesus is the Second Person of the Blessed Trinity.

_____ 5. Jesus is the model human being whom all should imitate.

_____ 6. Jesus is *the* man for others.

_____ 7. Jesus has conquered sin and death.

_____ 8. Jesus lives.

_____ 9. Jesus is love.

_____ 10. Jesus is my friend.

_____ 11. Jesus can be met today in prayer, in the sacraments, and in the scriptures.

_____ 12. Jesus can be met today in others, and in a special way in the poor and the outcast.

_____ 13. The church is the Body of Christ.

_____ 14. Prayer is a vital way to meet the living Lord.

_____ 15. Jesus loves me.

Reflection and Discussion: Add three statements to this list. Mark according to the same scale given above.

_____ a. _____

_____ b. _____

_____ c. _____

If you wish, share your responses with a friend.

JESUS AND YOU: TO KNOW IS TO LOVE

Why study about Jesus at this time in your life? A good question.

You live in a world that bombards you with many messages—often conflicting—about happiness and the meaning of life. You are also at the stage in your growth and development when you want to know what life means and where true happiness can be found.

Consider the words of Jesus:

"I am the Way, the Truth and the Life.
No one can come to the Father except through
    me" (Jn 14:6).

"I have come
so that they may have life
and have it to the full" (Jn 10:10).

Jesus claims to be the key to the mystery of life and to your own personal happiness. St. Paul used the following image to show the importance of the Lord in your life:

You are part of a building that has the apostles
and prophets for its foundations, and Christ Jesus
himself for its main cornerstone (Eph 2:20).

Paul's refreshing message announces the good news of Jesus. Jesus is the cornerstone on whom we should build our lives.

Contrast the promise of Jesus with the enticements of today. Drugs, material possessions, prestige, power, money and other pleasures are here today and gone tomorrow. We are tempted to rely on them, but can they bring us true happiness? As you read about and reflect on Jesus and his message, try to ask yourself if his good news might not be the key to the happiness and meaning you are seeking in your life now.

Knowledge of the Lord can help you to grow in love of the Lord. The musical *Godspell* contained the simple but beautiful song, "Day by Day." This prayer-song asks that we see the Lord more clearly, love him more dearly, and follow him more nearly. May your study of Jesus Christ help you to know the Lord so that you can love him with a fervent love and follow him with deep conviction.

OVERVIEW OF THE TEXT

Here is a chapter outline of the book to give you some idea of the themes that will be treated.

Chapter 1 looks at ways we can get back to the Jesus of history—Roman sources, Jewish sources, and especially the gospels.

Chapter 2 fills in some of the interesting historical details of Jesus' day and age.

Chapter 3 attempts to describe Jesus.

Chapter 4 presents the message of Jesus.

Chapter 5 shows how each of the gospel writers pictured Jesus.

Chapter 6 discusses the passion, death, resurrection and glorification of Jesus and explains the meaning of the paschal mystery in our lives.

Chapter 7 treats the titles of Jesus as a reflection of the faith of the early church.

Chapter 8 summarizes key teachings about Jesus which developed through the ages.

Chapter 9 discusses some current images of Jesus presented by theologians, the media, and the cults.

Chapter 10 shows where Jesus can be found in the world today, and how he calls each of us to holiness.

The Conclusion presents a brief "Jesus Catechism" and a short Bible Service you may use to conclude the course.

EXERCISE

Ask one of your parents or an adult you are close to to respond to the survey you took in this chapter (pages 8-9). Discuss his or her responses. Compare them with your own.

ONE

The Historical Jesus

Jesus Christ is the same today as he was yesterday and as he will be for ever.

—Hebrews 13:8

JESUS CHRIST! Two words: one a proper name, the other a lofty title. For Christians these are two of the most important words in human language. They are living words, faith words. They mean that God has broken into human history in a fantastic and unique way. As St. John records about Jesus:

"I am the Alpha and the Omega" says the Lord God, who is, who was, and who is to come, the Almighty (Rv 1:8).

This book discusses the beginning and end of all human life—Jesus Christ. The present chapter focuses on the historical evidence for Jesus' existence, looking at both non-Christian and Christian sources, especially the gospels which play a preeminent role in sketching out the portrait of Jesus and our theological understanding of him.

As we attempt to get back to the Jesus who lived almost 2,000 years ago, we are similar to Sherlock Holmes who had many mysteries to solve. But we should never forget that our task differs significantly from that of a detective. The man we seek is no ordinary man. We believe that in Jesus we can find the true meaning of our life. We must remember that in looking at the evidence for Jesus' existence we are not formulating a theory to solve just any mystery. Rather, we are searching for the Mystery of God's love present in human history, the Mystery that solves the very mystery of human existence.

WHAT'S IN A NAME?

We can begin our search for this person we call the Christ by looking at the meaning of his name. But before we do, pause and test your knowledge of the following Jewish names, all of which have profound significance.

NAMES AND MEANINGS

Directions: Match each name with its meaning. You will find the answers on the bottom of page 16.

_____ 1. Gabriel   a. Beloved

_____ 2. Ann   b. God is gracious

_____ 3. Michael   c. Princess

_____ 4. John   d. He who is like God

_____ 5. James   e. Let God add

_____ 6. Sarah   f. Full of grace, mercy and prayer

_____ 7. Joseph   g. God is mighty

_____ 8. Ruth   h. He will trip by the heel

_____ 9. David   i. A beautiful friend

Jesus, a common name in our Lord's day, was a late form of the Hebrew name Joshua (Yehoshua). The New Testament mentions a number of men with the name Jesus. St. Paul mentions a Jesus, known as the Just, who sent greetings to the Colossians. In the Acts of the Apostles, Luke writes of Elymas the Magician, a false prophet surnamed Bar-jesus, that is, the son of a man named Jesus. A final example appears in an old Greek manuscript of Matthew's gospel. Here Barabbas, the condemned criminal and insurrectionist, is known as Jesus. You might remember the scene where Pilate gave in to the pressure of the crowd when he posed the question: "Which one do you want me to release for you: [Jesus] Barabbas, or Jesus who is called Christ?" (Mt 27:17).

The literal meaning of the name Jesus is "Yahweh is salvation." Matthew refers to the significance of this name when he quotes the angel who speaks to Joseph in a dream:

> "She will give birth to a son and you must name
> him Jesus, because he is the one who is to save
> his people from their sins" (Mt 1:21).

We Christians believe that Jesus is indeed the Savior of the world.

Though the name Jesus was common in our Lord's day, it fell out of use by the end of the first century. Out of reverence for the holy name, Christians stopped calling their children by our Lord's name. *Jesus* became a sacred name, reserved in Christian devotion to the Lord himself. Jews stopped calling their boys by this name when it became clear to them that Christianity had become a separate religion. This probably took place during the rebellion of the Jews against the Romans in A.D. 66-70. Christians refused to fight in this war. As a result, the Jewish people felt betrayed and had little affection for the name of the founder of this new religion. Today, Spanish-speaking Christians sometimes name boys after our Lord. This practice is a cultural expression of devotion to Christ.

REFLECTION

In his letter to the Philippians, St. Paul quotes an early hymn concerning Jesus which greatly exalts his name:

> But God raised him high
> and gave him the name
> which is above all other names
> so that *all beings*
> in the heavens, on earth and in the underworld,
> *should bend the knee* at the name of Jesus
> and that every tongue should acclaim
> Jesus Christ as Lord,
> to the glory of God the Father (Phil 2:9-11)

This quotation suggests that we should greatly honor the name Jesus.

- What do you do to honor this name?

- What do you do when somebody misuses the name of Jesus?

Our Lord's last name, or surname, was not Christ. *Christ* is a title which means "Messiah" or "Anointed One." The title Christ is one of the most important titles the early church gave Jesus; it reflected what the early Christians believed about him. In Chapter 7 we will discuss this title in more detail along with some other important titles given our Lord.

What, then, may Jesus have been called to distinguish him from the other men of his day named Jesus? He would have been referred to by one of the following:

- *Jesus from Nazareth* or *Jesus the Nazarene.* It was typical to identify people by their place of residence. Nazareth was a small, hilly town in northern Palestine in the region known as Galilee. Many Jews of our Lord's day considered Nazareth a "hick" town. You might recall the sarcasm of Nathanael when he heard from Philip about Jesus of Nazareth: "From Nazareth? Can anything good come from that place?" (Jn 1:46).

- *Jesus the Carpenter.* A person was frequently designated by profession. One of the most common English surnames, Smith, designates a blacksmith or whitesmith (whitesmithing is a trade practiced by either a tinsmith or an ironworker who finishes iron rather than forges it). Mark's gospel informs us that Jesus worked as a carpenter before he began to preach.

- Jesus could have been known as *Jesus, the son of Joseph* or, in the Aramaic/Hebrew, *Jesus bar (ben) Joseph.* People were often known by their fathers' names. Mark alone designates Jesus by his mother's name, "the son of Mary" (Mk 6:3).

Answers to the quiz, "Names and Meanings":
1-g; 2-f; 3-d; 4-b; 5-h; 6-c; 7-e; 8-i; 9-a.

NEW TESTAMENT READING

Look at the family genealogies of Jesus given in Matthew 1:1-17 and Luke 3:23-38. The purpose of these family histories is theological. Note both the similarities and differences in the two accounts.

In both cases the genealogy of Jesus emphasizes his relationship to the whole human family. In addition, Matthew—who is writing to a Jewish-Christian audience—wants to show that Jesus is the fulfillment of the Old Testament prophecies made to the Jews which began with the covenant of God with Abraham. Thus Matthew traces Jesus' line to Abraham. Luke, writing to Christians who were Gentiles, traces Jesus to Adam, the father of the human race. Luke makes the theological point that Jesus is the Messiah of all people, Gentiles as well as Jews.

EVIDENCE FROM ROMAN SOURCES FOR JESUS' EXISTENCE

Is there any evidence for the existence of the historical Jesus outside of the New Testament? If we realize that Palestine was considered a minor though bothersome province in the large Roman Empire, we should not be surprised to find that there is very little written evidence by the Roman historians concerning Jesus.

But it was inevitable that some Romans would become aware of the existence of Jesus through the actions of his followers. These followers, known as Christians, claimed that the Jesus who had been put to death by the Roman prefect, Pontius Pilate, still lived. Their message, guided by the Holy Spirit, spread like wildfire across the Roman Empire. Three notable Roman writers—Suetonius, Tacitus and Pliny the Younger—mentioned Jesus or his followers.

Suetonius In the early part of the second century, the Roman author Suetonius compiled biographies of the first 12 Roman emperors, from Julius Caesar onward. In *Life of Claudius* he says of the emperor:

> He expelled the Jews from Rome on account of
> the riots in which they were constantly indulging,
> at the instigation of Chrestus.[1]

Suetonius erred in his retelling of the Jewish expulsion from Rome in A.D. 49 by assuming that Jesus was there. What probably happened was that when the early Christian missionaries went to the synagogues in Rome to tell the Jews that their long-awaited Messiah had come, they were met with such resistance that street riots resulted. Claudius believed that Christians and Jews were members of the same religious sect. He banished them both because of the civil disturbance that resulted from their infighting. Luke writes that when Paul arrived in Corinth in about A.D. 50,

> He met a Jew called Aquila whose family came
> from Pontus. He and his wife Priscilla had recently
> left Italy because an edict of Claudius had expelled
> all the Jews from Rome (Acts 18:2).

Tacitus   The Roman historian Tacitus writes in his *Annals* of the great fire which throught the city of Rome in A.D. 64. The Emperor Nero (stepson and successor to Claudius) probably was responsible for the fire and, to calm the anger of the Roman citizens against him, fixed the blame on the Christians. He burned many Christians and exposed others to the wild beasts. Tacitus, writing in A.D. 115-117, recounts the story of the fire and Nero's successful attempt to blame the Christians:

> They got their name from Christ, who was ex-
> ecuted by sentence of the procurator Pontius
> Pilate in the reign of Tiberius. That checked the
> pernicious superstition for a short time, but it
> broke out afresh—not only in Judaea, where the
> plague first arose, but in Rome itself, where all the
> horrible and shameful things in the world collect
> and find a home.[2]

---

1. Suetonius, *Claudius* 25.4 as cited by F. F. Bruce in *Jesus and Christian Origins Outside the New Testament* (Grand Rapids, Michigan: William B. Eerdmans Publishing Company, 1974), p. 21.

2. Tacitus, *Annals* 15.44 as cited by Donald Senior, C.P., in *Jesus: A Gospel Portrait* (Dayton: Pflaum, 1975), pp. 10-11.

Tacitus went out of his way to mention the origins of Christianity. Perhaps he checked official Roman records—possibly including Pontius Pilate's reports to Rome. Significantly, this is the only place in all ancient Roman histories where Pilate is mentioned, though the Jewish writers Philo and Josephus record his cruel rule in Judea.

Pliny the Younger   Pliny the Younger was a master letter writer. In A.D. 111 he was appointed imperial legate of the Roman province of Bithynia in northwest Asia Minor. He often wrote to the Roman emperor, Trajan. In one letter he asked the emperor how he should treat the ever-growing religious group known as Christians.

Pliny's letter and Trajan's reply are too lengthy to quote, but here are some interesting points: 1) Pliny mentioned that the "superstition" of Christianity had spread so rapidly that the pagan temples had fallen into disuse. Those who sold sacrificial animals were in serious economic trouble; 2) Pliny told the emperor that he freed Christians who rejected Christ and agreed to worship the pagan gods and the emperor, but that he condemned to death Christians who persisted in their beliefs about Jesus Christ; 3) Pliny recounted the Christian custom of celebrating the Eucharist on "a fixed day of the week."

Trajan's letter of response told Pliny that he had acted well in relation to the Bithynian Christians. He wrote that Pliny should punish any believing Christians who came to his attention, but also said that Pliny should not go looking for them. Trajan saw the Christians as potentially dangerous, but not so much a threat that they had to be hunted down like criminals.

Thus, while Roman historians make some references to Christ, usually in the context of his followers, their evidence for the historical Jesus is, at best, sketchy.

AN OUTSIDER'S VIEW

Discuss:

- How do you react to members of sects such as Hare Krishna, the Mormons or the Jehovah's Witnesses when they try to convert you? What is your impression of them? Do you sympathize with their cause? Why or why not? Can you as an outsider judge fairly the worth of a religious group?

- Relate the questions above to the way the Romans and Jews responded to the Christians.

Written Reflection: What would you say to an outsider who claims that Christians are nothing but hypocrites who don't truly live the teachings of their founder? Write a short essay responding to this accusation and share it with your classmates.

EVIDENCE FROM JEWISH SOURCES
FOR JESUS' EXISTENCE

Josephus   An interesting reference to Jesus comes from the colorful Jewish historian Josephus. Born around A.D. 37 Josephus commanded the Jewish forces in Galilee during the great revolt of A.D. 66-70. The Romans captured him, but because he predicted that the commander-in-chief of the Romans in Palestine, Vespasian, would one day be emperor, his life was spared. Vespasian did become emperor in A.D. 69, and Josephus became his friend.

Josephus composed a 20-volume history of the Jews. In this history Josephus tried to demonstrate to the Romans and to the Jew-hating emperor Domitian (A.D. 81-96) that the Jews were a noble people. In the 18th book he mentioned John the Baptist, calling him a good man. In the 20th book he noted that Annas the Younger—the son of the high priest mentioned in the gospels—put to death James the Just (A.D. 62), the leader of the Christian community in Jerusalem.

Of most interest to us, however, is Josephus' account of the troubles the Jews suffered under the governorship of Pontius Pilate (A.D. 26-36). Please study carefully the text which has been handed down to us:

> Now about this time lived Jesus, a wise man, if indeed he should be called a man. He was a doer of wonderful works, a teacher of men who receive the truth with pleasure, and won over many Jews and Greeks. He was the Christ. And when Pilate, at the information of the leading men among us, sentenced him to the cross, those who loved him at the start did not cease to do so, for he appeared to them alive again on the third day as had been foretold—both this and ten thousand other wonderful things concerning him—by the divine prophets. Nor is the tribe of Christians, so named after him, extinct to this day.[3]

---

3. Josephus, *Jewish Antiquities*, Vol. 18, as cited by Nahum N. Glatzer in *Jerusalem and Rome: The Writings of Josephus* (New York: Meridian Books, Inc., 1960), p. 145.

FOR ANALYSIS

Reread the passage from Josephus quoted above. Remember that Josephus was not a Christian.

1. Do you find it strange that a nonbeliever is the alleged author of this passage? Why or why not?
2. Can you suggest a theory about what might have happened as this passage was transmitted through the ages?

There is indeed a problem with the passage from Josephus. Scholars don't believe it comes entirely from Josephus because it sounds as though a believer wrote it. They theorize that certain passages which support Christian belief were added later by a Christian copyist, for example, the phrase "if indeed he should be called a man," and the references to Jesus as the Christ (Messiah) and to his resurrection. The church father Origen maintained that Josephus never accepted Christianity.

Regardless of what Josephus wrote or believed about Jesus, however, the significant point for our purposes is that he did not question the actual historical existence of Jesus.

Babylonian Talmud   Another reference to Jesus occurs in the Talmud, a commentary on Jewish law written down in the third century after Christ. This passage mentions a certain Yeshu (Jesus) who practiced magic and led Israel away from true Jewish worship. It also reports that this man had disciples and was "hanged on the eve of Passover."

FOR DISCUSSION

1. Does the scarcity of references to Jesus in Roman and Jewish material pose a problem for believers? Why or why not?
2. Does the evidence presented above make it easier for you to accept the historical Jesus? Why or why not?
3. As a class list some reasons why it is important that Jesus really existed.

THE EVIDENCE OF THE GOSPELS

The extrabiblical references tell us very little about Jesus, but it is reasonable to conclude that they refer to an actual, historical person, a man named Jesus who was put to death under Pontius Pilate during the reign of Tiberius. They also inform us that some of the Jewish leaders had a hand in his death, and that some of his followers regarded him as the Messiah, a lawgiver and the founder of a new way of life.

The writings of the New Testament, of course, are the strongest evidence for the existence of the historical Jesus. And it is from these writings, especially the gospels, that we learn the truth about this man who lived and preached in Palestine 20 centuries ago.

It is important to recognize, however, that a gospel is not a biography. A biography is a form of literature which attempts to tell the significant facts of a person's life. A well-written biography of your favorite sports hero, rock or movie star will satisfy your curiosity about the details of that person's life. The gospels don't do that. There are many things about the historical Jesus that we would like to know, but the gospel writers simply don't include that kind of information.

The gospels are summaries of faith, beautifully written theological statements of God's activity in the person of Jesus. They present the good news of Jesus (*gospel* means "good news"). They proclaim that God's kingdom is active in the world and that Jesus Christ is God's Son and the principal agent of that kingdom. They joyously announce that God loves us with incredible love and that Jesus died so that we may live and have eternal salvation. They spread the message that Jesus who was put to death now lives and has sent his Spirit to dwell in us. They describe what the early Christians held to be the most significant thing about Jesus, namely, that *Jesus is the gospel, Jesus is the good news.* In him we are reconciled to God. Historical facts are presented only as they support the saving activity of Jesus in his public life. And for all the gospels this saving activity is most acute in the passion, death and resurrection/glorification of the Lord.

THE JESUS OF HISTORY

A. *For Discussion:*

1. If you could ask Jesus one question about his life in Palestine, what would it be?

   Share your questions in class.

2. The gospels deal with good news. What is the *best* news that you could possibly hear? Share with your classmates. Is this good news related in any way to the summary of the good news which appears above? Explain.

B. *Images of Jesus.* The way we picture Jesus often tells more about us than it does about Jesus. For example, in the 1960s a "Wanted" poster was circulated showing a long-haired, bearded man in ragged clothes. The description read as follows:

JESUS CHRIST

Wanted—for sedition, criminal anarchy, vagrancy and conspiring to overthrow the established government.

Dresses poorly, *said* to be a carpenter by trade, ill-nourished, has visionary ideas, associates with common working people, the unemployed, and bums. *Alien*—believed to be a Jew. Professional agitator. Has red beard, marks on hands and feet the result of injuries inflicted by an angry mob led by respectable citizens and legal authorities.

1. Discuss what this description tells us about the people who wrote it. What are their values? What do they expect from a savior?

2. Compare the pictures of Jesus on pages 36, 118, 177, 190 and 195. How does each one depict him? Is he strong? regal? contemplative? gentle? joyful? caring? Why do you think these aspects were emphasized? Do some aspects of Jesus have special appeal to certain groups? to certain societies?

3. Find a picture which portrays Jesus for you—or draw your own. Write a description of Jesus and tape it under the picture. Share with your classmates.

THE FORMATION OF THE GOSPELS

The gospels do have something to say about the historical Jesus. But to understand how they do this we must first take a look at how they were formed.

Scripture scholars generally recognize that the gospels were developed in three distinct stages. They are the result of a gradual process of formation and composition. We can visualize these stages as follows.

Stage 1:	Stage 2:	Stage 3:
The historical —► Jesus	Oral preaching of —► the early church	The written gospels

Stage 1:
The Historical Jesus
The four gospels are rooted in the words and works of Jesus of Nazareth and in his interactions with his disciples and other groups of people he met during his public life. Scholars date the historical Jesus from his birth in 6-5 B.C. to his death in A.D. 30-33. Jesus must have been born before 4 B.C. because King Herod the Great's death occurred in that year. If we take Matthew's story about the slaughter of the Holy Innocents at face value, Jesus had to be born shortly before Herod's death.

Jesus' death had to take place within the 10-year span of Pilate's rule, A.D. 26-36. Matthew's gospel places his death at 3 o'clock on a Friday before Passover. Many scholars hold that this took place during the Jewish month of Nisan in the year A.D. 30 (April 7 on our calendar); recently, other scholars have set the date in April of the year A.D. 33.

A LITTLE GUY MAKES A BIG MISTAKE

You may have noticed that scholars place the date of our Lord's birth in the years we designate B.C.—*before* Christ. There is a simple explanation. Dionysius Exiguus (Denis the Little) was commissioned by the pope to change the Roman calendar—which was named after Julius Caesar and was dated from the founding of Rome in 753 B.C.—to a calendar starting with the birth of Jesus Christ. Dionysius made a mistake! His miscalculation was discovered centuries later, but it was too late to change all the official documents already dated.

Stage 2: Oral Preaching of the Early Church   Writing down the testimony about Jesus was not at the top of the list of activities of the early church. There were several reasons for this. First, writing takes effort and time. Second, people in those days learned best by hearing, not by reading.

After the appearances of Jesus to his disciples and the powerful gift of the Holy Spirit which enflamed Jesus' followers on Pentecost, the new Christians were burning with zeal to spread the good news of Jesus' victory over sin and death. Peter and especially Paul led the apostles in a burst of missionary activity that took the message of Jesus to every corner of the Mediterranean world.

Part of the earliest message was the belief that Jesus was to return in glory very shortly, during the lifetime of the apostles. Thus, a third reason why the gospels weren't written immediately:

It did not make much sense to write down eyewitness testimony if the world were to end soon. What would be the point of it? This mistaken belief even led some Christians to give up work. St. Paul wrote to the Thessalonians that those who didn't work should not get free meals from their Christian brothers and sisters.

The early Christian community kept the memory of Jesus alive by making collections of his sermons, parables, his great deeds (miracles) and his key sayings. The passion narrative and the resurrection appearances played key roles too. These collections—later to be used in composing the gospels—were used in the early liturgies, in the preaching of the good news to nonbelievers and in the additional instructions given to new con-

Pentecost, by El Greco (detail)

verts. With eyewitnesses and close disciples still alive and pro-claiming what they had seen and experienced in Jesus, no one thought that it was important to write down a biography of Jesus. The important thing was to proclaim the good news of salvation and God's great love for us in his Son, Jesus Christ.

Why were the gospels finally written? St. Paul gives us a hint in this important passage written to the Galatians sometime be-tween A.D. 52 and 57:

> Not that there can be more than one Good News; it is merely that some troublemakers among you want to change the Good News of Christ; and let me warn you that if anyone preaches a version of the Good News different from the one we have already preached to you, whether it be ourselves or an angel from heaven, he is to be condemned. I am only repeating what we told you before: if anyone preaches a version of the Good News dif-ferent from the one you have already heard, he is to be condemned (Gal 1:7-9).

Somebody was distorting the true gospel; thus, something had to be done to create a permanent record of what God the Father really accomplished through his Son.

An additional reason for writing the gospels was very prac-tical: The eyewitnesses were beginning to die or be put to death. The early Christians were in fact wrong about the early return of Jesus. To preserve the authentic testimony the good news of Jesus had to be committed to writing.

SCRIPTURE HUNT # 1

1. Read Matthew 2 and Luke 3:1-23. Scholars use both of these passages to date Jesus.

   Information:
   - Herod was king of Judea, Idumea and Samaria from 37 B.C. to 4 B.C.
   - By Roman dating, the 15th year of Tiberius' reign went from August to August, A.D. 28-29; by the Syrian method of dating, it was from September/October, A.D. 27-28.

Questions:

    a. How old was Jesus when he began to preach?_____

    b. Should Luke 3:23 be taken literally?_____

2. Read Acts 2:14-41. This represents the heart of the oral preaching of the early church, called the *kerygma*—the core teaching about Jesus. Make a brief outline of the major points in this teaching.

Stage 3:
The Written Gospels

There is only one gospel, and that is the person of Jesus Christ. He is the good news of God's great love for us. But the church recognizes four faith expressions of this good news, that is, four written gospels. These four gospels are 1) authentic testimonies of faith in Jesus; 2) inspired; 3) written; and 4) communal expressions of the good news of Jesus.

Three of the gospels—Matthew, Mark and Luke—are closely related and are called the *synoptic gospels.* When Matthew and Luke composed their versions of the good news, they relied on a version of Mark's gospel. When we line up Mark, Matthew and Luke in parallel columns, we can note many similarities; indeed they can be "read together." Hence the term *synoptic* (from the Greek words *syn*—"together" and *optic*—"look at").

John's gospel was the last written, most highly developed theologically, and not directly dependent on any of the other gospels.

The chart that follows gives a bird's-eye view of the gospels. The theological slant of each gospel differs because the gospels were composed by different people writing at different times and in different places. Each gospel reflects the particular insights of the gospel writer. Furthermore, each gospel was written to and for a particular Christian community and is tailored to meet the concerns of that community. All the gospels present the good news of Jesus, but they adapt their presentation to the religious needs of the intended audience. With these points in mind, please study the following diagram. It is worth noting that the authorship of each gospel is still disputed.

GOSPEL	AUTHOR	DATE	INTENDED AUDIENCE	MAJOR THEOLOGICAL SLANT
Mark	John Mark, a close follower of Peter, perhaps his secretary	shortly after the death of Peter (A.D. 64), as early as A.D. 65 or perhaps as late as A.D. 70	Christians, especially those trying to understand "suffering in Christ" the Romans	centers around the titles "Christ" and "Son of Man" meaning of suffering
Matthew	author unknown, possibly a former Jewish scribe a collection of sayings compiled in Aramaic by the apostle Matthew was probably used as a source	sometime after the destruction of the Temple in Jerusalem by the Romans in A.D. 70, probably A.D. 75-85	a Jewish-Christian audience	Jesus is the expected Messiah-king promised to the Jews
Luke	Luke, a physician, the secretary of St. Paul	suggested dates range from A.D. 75 to 85	a Gentile-Christian audience	Christianity is a religion for all persons depicts Jesus' concern for all humanity by identification with the poor, outcasts, etc.
John	probably written and edited by very close disciples of St. John the Apostle, the "beloved disciple"	sometime in the last decade of the first century	the Christian churches established around the Roman Empire	Jesus is the Messiah. He is superior to all the prophets, including John the Baptist religious belief and practice should be rooted in Jesus Christ

THE JESUS OF HISTORY

We conclude this chapter with several questions: Can we backtrack through the process which produced the gospels and discover a historical Jesus behind them? Can we leap back over the 35-70 years of oral tradition and demonstrate that a unique person is behind the gospels? Can we indeed get to the first stage—the stage of the historical Jesus—when all we have to work with are the written documents from the third stage? Can we demonstrate that this Jesus written about in the gospels existed, and that he is not the invention of the early church or the gospel writers?

The answer to all these questions is yes. We can know with a good deal of certitude that Jesus did exist, and that the later preaching about him and the written gospels are firmly rooted in his actual existence. Questions about what he was like as a teacher, friend, savior, God-made-man, and the like will be addressed in later chapters.

Discovering the Jesus of History: Methods and Examples

Scholars have developed some interesting tests or methods which strongly indicate the existence of the historical Jesus. Three of them are discussed here: 1) originality, 2) consistency of content, and 3) linguistic analysis.

Originality   If the gospels report something as coming from Jesus—for example, a saying or an event—and it can't be attributed to either the Jews of his day or to the early

Christian community, then it must originate with Jesus.

- *Abba:* Abba is an Aramaic word, the language that Jesus spoke. It means "daddy," a word usually translated as "father." Its significance? First we have to realize that when the Jews of our Lord's day addressed a prayer to God, they used terms of great respect. A typical Jewish address to God in prayer was "Master of Heaven and Earth." They always used some lofty title when praying to God because they wanted to emphasize that God was so great, so divine, and that they were mere creatures compared to him. They would never dare to address God so intimately as "daddy."

  Yet *Abba* is precisely the word Jesus used when he prayed to God. Only God's Son could have the freedom to make bold use of such a term. Nobody else did. No one would have dared! Furthermore, Jesus invited his followers to address God as Abba. In doing so, he revolutionized religion. The almighty God is our loving Father, an intimate daddy who will care for us with incredible love.

- *Amen:* Amen is a Hebrew word which means "certainly." It was always used at the end of an oath or a blessing or a curse or some similar saying. It showed agreement with the words of another.

  But Jesus used it to introduce, not end, his own words, "Amen, amen, I say. . . ." This way of speaking was so new and unusual that the gospel writers retained it when they recorded the words of Jesus. John uses it 25 times in his gospel. Nobody but Jesus taught this way. It meant that he spoke with unusual authority and quoted no other teacher. He is the unique source of this way of speaking.

- *Parables*: While other rabbis of Jesus' day used poetic language, scripture scholars can find nothing in the writings of St. Paul or the rabbis or in the writings of the Essenes (see next chapter) or any other Old or New Testament writer to compare to the way Jesus used parables. The gospels contain 41 parables which Jesus used to convey the essentials of his message.

Consistency of Content   A strong argument for the historical Jesus is that the small units found in the gospels—for example, parables, sayings, miracle stories, ethical teachings—are consistent with one another and coincide with the larger, overall picture that arises from reading the gospels as a whole.

- *Jesus and love:* Jesus taught his followers that they should love their enemies and pray for their persecutors. This message of love was not a popular one then (nor is it especially popular today). It appears as the theme of several parables, in his dealings with the outcasts of his day, in the Sermon on the Mount and—most dramatically—in his own prayer to God the Father to forgive his tormentors as he hung on the cross.

- *Sacrifice:* In many places Jesus asks his followers to sacrifice for him and others. For example, Jesus says,

  > "Anyone who finds his life will lose it;
  > anyone who loses his life for my sake will
  > find it" (Mt 10:39).

Jesus not only preached this theme, he himself lived it. He consistently lived what he preached. This argues for an authentic and unique person behind the gospels.

Linguistic Analysis   Some scholars have painstakingly taken all the words attributed to Jesus and translated them from the Greek back into his mother tongue, Aramaic. (The gospels were written in Greek.) This study has detected some remarkable patterns of speech in the Jesus of history which show that he was not just another rabbi (teacher) of his day. These consistent and repeated speech patterns can only lead us to conclude that there was a unique, special and creative teacher: Jesus of Nazareth. Examples include poetic rhythms that make his speech easy to memorize, puns, riddles, striking paradoxes, use of the phrase "kingdom of God" and similar techniques.

It is reasonable to conclude from the evidence that there was a Jesus of Nazareth, and that he was quite a remarkable person!

FOR REFLECTION

1. What does a father's love mean to you?_____

   _____

2. What does a mother's love mean to you?_____

   _____

Discuss the difference between the two.

3. What is the difference between calling someone "Daddy" and calling him "Father"?

   _____

   _____

4. What does it mean to you to be able to call God, Abba?

   _____

   _____   _____

SUMMARY

Here is a short summary of the key points in this chapter:

1. Our Lord's name, Jesus, means "Yahweh saves" and symbolizes what Christ has done and continues to do for us.

2. There is some evidence outside the New Testament for the existence of Jesus, but it is very limited. Some Roman and Jewish writers either allude to him or mention his followers. The following offer some evidence for his existence: Suetonius, Tacitus, Pliny the Younger, Josephus, and the Babylonian Talmud.

3. Our primary source of knowledge about Jesus is the New Testament. The gospels are faith summaries which record the good news of Jesus as Savior of all of us.

4. The gospels resulted from three stages of development which spanned a period of years. These stages were:

    a. the historical life of Jesus (6-4 B.C. — A.D. 30-33)

    b. the early preaching of the church (A.D. 30 — the first gospel)

    c. the written gospels themselves (A.D. 65-100)

5. The gospels are the strongest historical evidence that Jesus existed. A careful study of them reveals a unique teacher who lived a life consistent with what he preached. This teacher taught a message of love, addressed God as Abba, used Amen to begin his sayings, conveyed key teachings in parables, and used many other devices that made him stand out among the teachers of his day.

EXERCISE

1. Please read Mark 2-3.

2. What was the most difficult verse for you to understand in these chapters of Mark? _____

3. Write your favorite verse here: _____

    _____

    _____

4. What would you say these verses reveal about Jesus?

    _____

    _____

5. What verse helped you the most? _____

    Why? _____

    _____

Share and discuss your research and answers.

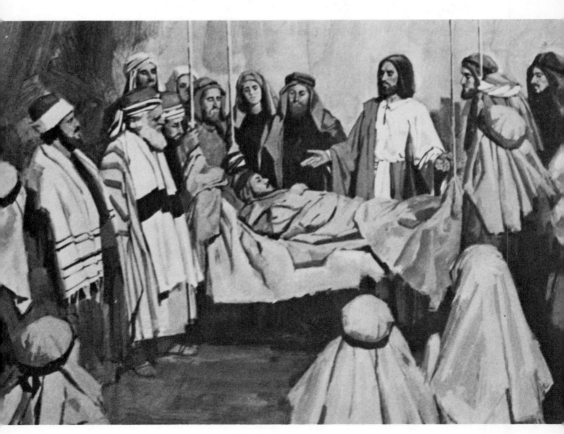

SCRIPTURE REFLECTION

Something which has existed since the beginning,
that we have heard,
and we have seen with our own eyes;
that we have watched
and touched with our hands:
the Word, who is life—
this is our subject.
That life was made visible:
we saw it and we are giving our testimony,
telling you of the eternal life
which was with the Father and has been made visible
      to us.
What we have seen and heard
we are telling you
so that you too may be in union with us,
as we are in union
with the Father
and with his Son Jesus Christ.
We are writing this to make our own joy complete
      (1 Jn 1:1-4).

TWO

The Everyday World of Jesus

I am the good shepherd;
I know my own
and my own know me,
Just as the Father knows me,
and I know the Father;
and I lay down my life for my sheep.
—John 10:14-15

Jesus lived the life of a Palestinian Jew of the first century. If we want to know the Jesus of history, we must have a basic knowledge of the world in which he lived. This chapter will examine Jesus' world by looking at a short history of his people and by examining the political situation of his day. It will also look at the geography of Palestine and discuss some of the customs and practices of our Lord's day. Finally, the chapter will briefly discuss the various groups of Jews which were active early in the first century. These groups are important because Jesus had to deal with their views about how God interacts with his people.

QUIZ ON JESUS' WORLD

Directions: How much do you know about Jesus' world? Here are a few questions to test your basic knowledge.

1. What would Jesus most likely have eaten as the basic food at each meal?

_____ a. lamb

_____ b. eggs

_____ c. bread

_____ d. salad greens

2. What great act of love by Yahweh on behalf of the Jews formed them as a people and is celebrated even today in the Passover feast?

_____ a. the covenant with Abraham

_____ b. the Exodus experience

_____ c. the return of the Jews from the Babylonian Captivity

_____ d. the rule of the Maccabees

3. Which Jewish group did not believe in the resurrection of the dead?

_____ a. Zealots

_____ b. Essenes

_____ c. Pharisees

_____ d. Sadducees

4. In what province of Palestine is Bethlehem located?

_____ a. Galilee

_____ b. Samaria

_____ c. Judea

_____ d. Perea (Transjordan)

5. What language did Jesus speak?

_____ a. Greek

_____ b. Aramaic

_____ c. Hebrew

_____ d. Arabic

(Answers can be found on page 43.)

THE STORY OF THE CHOSEN PEOPLE

We are a historical people, so God chose to begin to reveal himself at a certain time and with a certain people. This starting point was approximately 4000 years ago; the person he chose was a wandering herdsman, a man of faith by the name of Abraham. We can divide the first 2000 years of the history of these people chosen by God into nine parts:

1. Abraham's Call (c. 1900 B.C.)

Yahweh called Abraham from the desert in order to create a people, his Chosen People. As Abraham's grandson said, and all Jews from then on have proudly affirmed:

> "My father was a wandering Aramaean. He went down into Egypt to find refuge there, few in numbers; but there he became a nation, great, mighty, and strong" (Dt 26:5).

Abraham's courageous faith in following the word of God and leaving the life he had known resulted in God blessing him with a family and a land, and this when Abraham was a very old man. His grandson Jacob (later given the name Israel) reared a family north of Palestine, but one of Jacob's sons, Joseph, was sold into Egypt as a slave. Joseph's intelligence got him the job of prime minister in Egypt. His position of influence enabled him to settle his family in northeastern Egypt when there was a famine in their native land. Jacob's descendents, the Israelites, grew in number but became feared by the Egyptians and were forced to do hard labor.

2. The Exodus Experience (c. 1250 B.C.)

The Exodus was *the* great event in Jewish history. Under the leadership of their able prophet and leader, Moses, the Chosen People were delivered from slavery in Egypt. This incredible event, without parallel in history, revealed to the Israelites that their God—Yahweh—was a God of unlimited love. All later generations of Jews have commemorated the Exodus event in the great feast of Passover.

God's love manifested in the Exodus experience freed the Israelites from slavery and gave them new life. His care for them in the Sinai desert showed them that he would forever sustain them and keep them in his loving care. In turn, God asked that they live the kind of life that would show the rest of the world that they were God's people. They were to do this by consciously witnessing to the worship of the one true God and by living the Ten Commandments which God had given to Moses on Mount Sinai.

3. Entry Into the Promised Land (c. 1200 B.C.)

Yahweh's selection of the Chosen People and his protection, care and love for them formed half of an open-ended contract known as a *covenant*. The Israelites for their part were to accept God's love and live a life of commitment to him. God never failed to uphold his part of the covenant; for example, after freeing the Chosen People from slavery in Egypt, he gave them a nation. This took place when Joshua led the Israelites into the land of Canaan. There the Israelites settled on the mountainsides with their cattle, sheep and goats, and gradually captured the surrounding Canaanite villages and towns.

LOOKING AT THE JEWISH STORY

The story of the Jews in the Hebrew scriptures is the story of Jesus' people. Our Lord knew it well and treasured it as his heritage. Read the following passages and answer the questions given:

Abraham: Genesis 12, 15, 17

1. What covenant did God make with Abraham?

_____

2. What was the sign of this covenant?

_____

Moses: Exodus 19-20

3. What covenant did God make on Sinai?

_____

4. Write the first three commandments (in a shortened form) as they appear in your bible:

_____

_____

_____

Joshua: Joshua 3,6

5. Describe two marvelous deeds Yahweh accomplished for the Jews which are described in these chapters:

_____

_____

4. Creation of a Monarchy (c. 1020 B.C.)

Not too long before 1000 B.C. the enterprising Israelites became powerful enough to set up their own government. Saul, their first king, led them to victory against the Canaanites and other neighboring tribes. King David, his successor, captured the important city of Jerusalem and built his palace there. David gained the admiration and respect of the neighboring nations and became the symbol of Jewish military might and glory. Later generations looked to his rule as the Golden Age of Jewish political power.

After David's son Solomon built the first Temple, Jewish political power declined. From around 922 B.C., when the country was split into the northern kingdom of Israel and the southern kingdom of Judah, the Chosen People yearned for a unified nation under a strong leader. Their hopes centered on the prophecies concerning a great leader-king, or Messiah, who would re-establish a strong, peaceful nation. They based their hopes on Yahweh's promise to send a Messiah who would establish his kingdom on earth.

Answers to "Quiz on Jesus' World":
1-c; 2-b; 3-d; 4-c; 5-b.

KING DAVID

Directions: Read 2 Samuel 7:8-16 and answer the following questions:

1. What did David do before he became a king?

_____

2. Which two verses in this section did the Jews look to as God's promise of a Messiah?

_____

Reflection. The Jews believe that King David composed the Psalms. Prayerfully read one of the most famous of these prayer-songs, Psalm 104.

5. Fall of the Northern Kingdom to the Assyrians (722 B.C.)

The divided kingdom soon became prey to the enemies of the Israelites. The northern kingdom suffered many internal strifes with resulting changes in dynasty. Finally, in 722 B.C., Assyria, its powerful eastern neighbor, conquered it. Most of its people were resettled in Mesopotamia where they were soon absorbed by the Assyrians.

When the Assyrians overran the northern kingdom, they left behind the crippled, the blind, the sick, the elderly and a few who were able to hide. Emigrants from Assyria intermarried with these remnant Jews. These people became known as Samaritans, named for Samaria, the chief city of the region. The Samaritans adopted pagan customs and only gradually returned to the worship of the one true God.

During this time of strife Yahweh sent prophets to interpret for the Chosen People what was happening to them and why. The prophet Hosea spoke of Yahweh's justice in punishing an unfaithful Israel, an Israel that had fallen into the worship of false gods (idolatry). But Hosea also reminded his people that Yahweh is a passionate lover who will forever remain faithful to his beloved, Israel.

HOSEA

Read Hosea 2-3 to get a flavor of how this prophet portrayed God's love for his people.

6. Fall of the Southern Kingdom and the Exile (587-537 B.C.)

For a while, the southern kingdom fared better than the northern, but in 587 B.C. Nebuchadnezzar captured Jerusalem. This event began the period known as the Babylonian Captivity and marked a low point in Jewish national history. The vast majority of people were deported to Babylonia where they were relatively well-treated. They were permitted to practice their religion and to maintain a separate ethnic identity. The prophet Ezekiel and the writer-prophet known as Second Isaiah promised on behalf of Yahweh that the Chosen People would eventually return to the Promised Land:

> Do not be afraid, for I am with you.
> I will bring your offspring from the east,
> and gather you from the west.
> To the north I will say, "Give them up"
> and to the south, "Do not hold them" (Is 43:5-6).

In 538 B.C. Cyrus of Persia overran Babylonia. He permitted captured peoples to return to their homelands. Many of those who considered the southern kingdom of Judah their home did return. A large number probably remained along the Tigris and Euphrates rivers because the soil was more fertile there. Since those who returned to Palestine were nearly all people whose parents and grandparents had come from Judah, the group became known as Jews.

THE SUFFERING SERVANT

The writings of Second Isaiah played an important part in Jesus' own ministry. These writings encouraged the Jews in captivity because of their promise that God would eventually redeem them from their sufferings. They told the downtrodden Jews that God would raise up a servant through whose sufferings people would attain salvation.

Read Isaiah 52:13—53:12. Christians believe that this "Suffering Servant Song" applies perfectly to Jesus. Find three points from this passage that could be applied to our Lord and list them below.

1. _____

2. _____

3. _____

7. Return, Rebuilding of the Temple, and Renewal of the Covenant (537-428 B.C.)

Under the new leader Zerubbabel and two prophets, Haggai and Zechariah, the Temple was rebuilt in Jerusalem (520-516 B.C.). The Jews were still having trouble with the Samaritans and other neighbors. Their city still lay in ruins. But Nehemiah rebuilt the city, and the priest and scribe Ezra restored and renewed the ancient religion.

Palestine was relatively peaceful under the Persians. This lasted for about 200 years until the Greek, Alexander the Great, conquered this part of the world. In the midst of this new turmoil, the Jews remained strong in their conviction that a Messiah-king would re-establish their former political glory. They held firm to the prophecy of Jeremiah who wrote during the Exile that Yahweh would establish a new covenant:

> No, this is the covenant I will make with the House of Israel when those days arrive—it is Yahweh who speaks. Deep within them I will plant my Law, writing it on their hearts. Then I will be their God and they shall be my people (Jer 31:33).

8. Tribulations Under the Greeks (332-175 B.C.)

In 332 B.C., the dashing Alexander the Great conquered

Palestine. Though he lived only to the age of 33, he brought to Palestine Greek culture and thought. His successors, the Ptolemies of Egypt, exiled a large number of Jews to Egypt. Generally speaking, though, the Jews prospered under this new regime although they had to pay exorbitant taxes.

The Seleucids of Syria succeeded the Ptolemies. The worst of these rulers was Antiochus IV who hated the Jews and considered them dangerous enemies. He attacked Jerusalem on the Sabbath knowing that the true believers would not fight on that day. He gave orders that Greek gods be worshiped. He forbade the Jews to observe the Sabbath. Nor was circumcision (the sign of the covenant with Abraham) permitted. Copies of Hebrew scriptures were destroyed. In December of 168 B.C. sinful heathen rites took place in the Temple courts and—worst of all from a Jewish standpoint—a pig was sacrificed on the holy altar. The Jews considered this a "disastrous abomination" (Dn 11:31) because an unclean people offered an unclean animal.

9. The Maccabean Revolt and Hasmonean Rule (164 B.C.- 63 B.C.)

Despite all the political oppression outlined above, the Jews had always enjoyed religious freedom until Antiochus. In reaction to this man's oppression the Maccabeus family led a revolt which eventually led to self-rule for almost a century under the Hasmoneans (the original name of the Maccabeus family). Political instability characterized this dynasty which was occupied with fending off the Syrians and establishing an acceptable line of rulers.

This period of political autonomy ended when the Roman general Pompey captured Jerusalem in 63 B.C. (Not until 1948 and the establishment of the new Jewish state of Israel was Palestine to again be under the control of the Chosen People.) The Romans controlled the area of Palestine for several centuries after Pompey's victory. It was during this Roman rule that Jesus the Christ, the King of Kings, was born.

GOD PROTECTS HIS PEOPLE

A list of the oppressors of the Jews throughout the Old Testament period would include the following:

> Egyptians
> Canaanites
> Assyrians
> Babylonians
> Persians
> Greeks
> Ptolemies (the Egyptians)
> Seleucids (the Syrians)
> Romans

Discuss:

1. Explain how the Jews survived in the midst of all these turmoils.
2. What is the primary nature of God's covenant promise to the Jews? (Is it self-rule? survival? a sense of national identity? etc.)
3. Imagine the flurry Jesus made when he came on the scene. Read Mark 11:1-11. Study verses 9-10. What might some people have thought of Jesus at this point in his ministry? Explain.

PALESTINE UNDER ROMAN RULE

Throughout his public ministry Jesus had to contend with the realities of foreign oppression. Like his fellow Jews, Jesus was quite aware of the Roman presence in his homeland. Eventually he was brought before the Romans and charged with being a threat to the emperor's authority. This crime, of course, was punishable by death.

Several officials of the Roman occupation are mentioned in the New Testament. Among these, the most important are Herod the Great, Herod Antipas and Pontius Pilate.

Herod the Great   Herod the Great was from Idumea. A non-Jew, he accepted Greek customs and practices. By virtue of his ruthlessness he won kingship over all Palestine. A vindictive and suspicious man, he killed his eldest sons for fear that they might usurp his throne. Thus, the slaughter of the Holy Innocents at the time of Jesus' birth would have been in character for this man.

Herod was hated by the Jews. His pagan practices (for example, he had 10 wives) and cruel, bloodthirsty rule alienated his subjects. Herod was a friend of the Roman emperor, Caesar Augustus. The emperor allowed Herod to rule Palestine but had a keen insight into his character when he remarked that it would be better to be Herod's pig than his son.

Herod was one of the great builders of the ancient world. He rebuilt Caesarea with an artificial harbor, and it became one of the great ports of the Mediterranean world. In addition, partly to win favor with the Jews, he undertook to rebuild the Jerusalem Temple along the scale of Solomon's Temple. This massive project began in 20 B.C. and was not completed until A.D. 66, only four years before the Romans leveled it.

The Temple Herod began was beautiful and the pride of the Jewish nation. Jesus himself was proud of the Temple and knew that it represented the center of the Jewish nation, the symbol of its contact with the divine. But imagine the ridicule he must have suffered when his opponents misinterpreted his words:

> "Destroy this sanctuary, and in three days I will raise it up." The Jews replied, "It has taken forty-six years to build this sanctuary: are you going to raise it up in three days?" But he was speaking of the sanctuary that was his body (Jn 2:19-21).

Pontius Pilate   Herod the Great died in 4 B.C. His will divided his kingdom among three of his sons: Archelaus, Herod Antipas and Philip. Archelaus inherited Idumea, Judea and Samaria which he ruled for 10 years until, because of his cruelty, he was banished to Gaul. At that time Rome decided that Samaria, Judea and Idumea should be under the direct control of Rome and not delegated to a king-designate. (Check the map on page 54 for the location of these territories.) Thus in A.D. 6 a Roman procurator was appointed. This procurator was under the authority of the governor of Syria. The fifth procurator was Pontius Pilate, who ruled from A.D. 26-36.

Pilate was stationed on the coast at Caesarea but came to Jerusalem for the great Jewish feasts. His presence was meant to discourage any possible rebellion. Besides keeping peace the procurator collected taxes, made periodic reports to Rome, and handled court cases involving capital offenses because the Jewish courts were not allowed to sentence anyone to death.

The Jews despised Pilate. When the Jewish leaders turned Jesus over to Pilate and asked that he be executed, Pilate tried to evade responsibility by sending him to Herod Antipas. Eventually, however, Pilate did sentence Jesus to death.

Herod Antipas   Another son of Herod the Great was named Herod Antipas. He ruled Galilee and Perea (Transjordan) throughout the hidden life and public ministry of Jesus. Apparently Herod Antipas made no serious attempt to arrest Jesus during his ministry, but he did have spies who reported

Jesus' activities. Jesus called Herod a fox when warned by some Pharisees that Herod was trying to kill him. As a Galilean, Jesus was under Herod's jurisdiction and appeared before him during his trial.

Like his father, Herod Antipas was a builder. He constructed the new city of Tiberias on the western shore of the Sea of Galilee, naming it after the emperor Tiberius. The gospels do not tell us if Jesus ever entered this city.

Herod fell into disfavor with the Jews when he divorced his wife and married Herodias, his niece and the wife of his half-brother. John the Baptist's railing against this marriage led to his arrest and execution. In A.D. 39 Herod Antipas was exiled to Gaul.

HEROD ANTIPAS AND PILATE

Read Mark 6:17-29. Did Herod Antipas really want to kill John the Baptist? Why or why not?

Read Matthew 27:11-26. Did Pilate wish to crucify Jesus? Why or why not?

Discuss: In what way were Herod and Pilate alike? What basic personality flaw did they show? In what ways may we be tempted to act as they did when it is our turn to do the right thing? Give examples.

THE JEWS AND ROMAN RULE

Most of Jesus' fellow Jews despised the Romans even though Rome was relatively tolerant of the Jews. For example, Jews were not conscripted into the Roman army. Why, then, did most Jews hate the Romans? Undoubtedly because the Jews were convinced that no one else had the right to rule God's Chosen People. Only Yahweh was their king. Rome ruled the world—and thus naturally she conflicted with Jewish hopes.

It is true that Rome allowed a degree of self-rule. Each community in Palestine had its own council. For Judea there was the Great Council, known as the Sanhedrin. It had the freedom to make numerous laws, hold trials and administer its decisions, though Rome reserved the right of capital punishment.

Rome, however, controlled the selection of candidates for the office of high priest, and part of the time even kept charge of the high priest's robes, a desecration of sacred things in the eyes of the Jews.

The Jews also hated to pay the taxes Rome required of its subjects, even though Rome spent most of Palestine's direct taxes, like the land taxes, on physical improvements in the province itself—building roads, aqueducts and the like. It was the matter of internal revenue, or customs, that provoked the Jews. Even on a short journey the traveler had to pass numerous tax collection points. The right to collect these taxes went to the highest bidder. Almost all the tax collectors, called *publicans,* abused their power by bribing procurators and exacting exorbitant rates. The Jews felt that this money belonged to God and could be spent better in the Temple. Jews who worked as publicans were considered robbers, certainly no better than prostitutes, and were despised by all. Imagine the shock to the Pharisees when Jesus associated with these hated men.

The Jews of our Lord's day, then, suffered under Roman occupation, and many people hoped for a Messiah-king who would rid the Promised Land of the oppressive foreigners.

PUBLICANS

Read Luke 18:9-14. What would the ordinary Jew of Jesus' day have thought when he heard this parable? What point is Jesus making?

Read Matthew 10:2-5. Memorize the list of apostles. What is the significance of Matthew?

PALESTINE: THE LAND

Palestine means "land of the Philistines." The Philistines occupied the coastal areas and ruled the land until King David defeated them. The gospels tell us the major provinces of this land in Jesus' day:

> Large crowds followed him, coming from Galilee, the Decapolis, Jerusalem, Judaea and Transjordania (Mt 4:25).

Study the map on page 54. It shows the principal places mentioned in the gospels. Note that Galilee is in the north, Judea in the south and Samaria sandwiched in between. A few points are worth noting about each region.

The inhabitants from Judea were mostly the descendents of the Jews who had returned from Babylonia. Most of the population clustered around Jericho and Jerusalem, the holy city which was the center of Jewish worship in the Temple. The Jews in this area were fanatical about their religion and tended to look down on Jews from other regions as less religious. The area around the Dead Sea and the southern part of Judea was mostly desert.

Galilee also contained a mostly Jewish population, but a population that frequently came in contact with non-Jews. Thus, Galilee had a more cosmopolitan outlook. Galileans spoke a dialect and tended to be looked down on by Jews from Jerusalem. Galilee was more fertile and prosperous than Judea.

The shortest route between Galilee in the north and Judea in the south took the traveler through Samaria. The Jews of our Lord's day did not allow Samaritans to worship in Jerusalem. Hostility continually festered between the Jews and the Samaritans. The pious Jew of Jesus' day would not associate with a Samaritan. Jesus passed through Samaria on numerous occasions. He shocked his apostles by speaking to a Samaritan woman in public. Furthermore, to show that his Father's love included even the hated enemy, Jesus made a Samaritan the hero of one of his parables on love.

THE GOOD SAMARITAN

Read Luke 10:29-37.

What is the theme of the parable? _____

Rewrite this parable using an example your classmates could relate to. Share these.

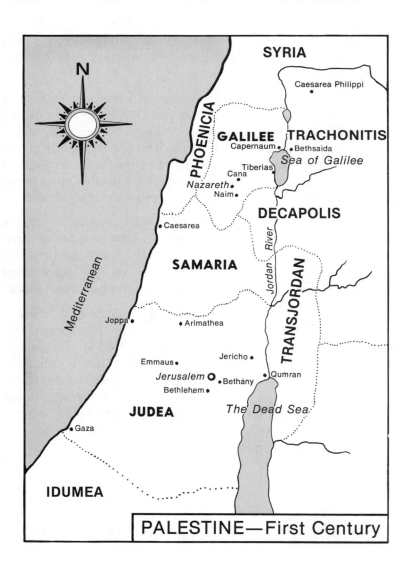

PALESTINE—First Century

DAILY LIFE IN JESUS' DAY

Language

Jesus spoke Aramaic, the language of his people. Hebrew was the classical language of the Jews, but most Jews did not speak or understand Hebrew even though most of their scriptures were written in that sacred language.

As a Semitic language, Aramaic used certain speech forms to express meaning. Here are three examples that will help us understand Jesus and his message better.

Parallel statements Semitic languages frequently express an important thought a second time in a slightly different form. Both forms are complete expressions; they say the same thing. Jesus used this form when he said,

"Give to anyone who asks, and if anyone wants to borrow, do not turn away" (Mt 5:42).

Comparisons Except for Arabic, the Semitic languages do not possess a special way to express the comparative and superlative degrees; they don't have equivalents of our words *better* and *best*. Thus, they have to express comparison in other ways. Jesus, quoting the Old Testament, told his followers,

"You have learnt how it was said: *You must love your neighbor* and hate your enemy" (Mt 5:43).

The meaning of this Old Testament teaching was that the Jews should love their neighbor (fellow Jews) *more than* the enemy. The Old Testament was not saying that the Jews should literally hate their enemies, but rather that their obligation was first to their fellow Jews. Jesus, of course, changed this teaching. He said,

"Love your enemies and pray for those who persecute you" (Mt 5:44).

Exaggeration Use of hyperbole, exaggeration to make a point, was common in Jewish speech. English also has this technique—*This suitcase weighs a ton* or *That exam*

is going to kill me are examples—but doesn't use it as frequently as the Aramaic. Exaggerated statements are not meant to be taken literally. When Jesus said,

> "You blind guides! Straining out gnats and swallowing camels!" (Mt 23:24)

he was making the point that while the Pharisees concentrated on the small faults of others they missed their own major sins. He exaggerated to drive home his message.

Some Latin was probably used in Palestine because of the occupying Roman troops. However, by the first century Greek was the common language of the Empire. Jewish merchants and others who dealt with foreigners spoke Greek. The early Christians wrote their letters and gospels in the common Greek (called *koine*) because that language was universally spoken throughout the Roman Empire.

A MANNER OF SPEAKING

Read Matthew 5:29. Which of the three speech techniques discussed above does it exemplify? Are we to take this passage literally? Why or why not?

A Point of Interest. Look at a crucifix. Does it have the insignia *INRI* written at the top? What does *INRI* mean? It was customary for Roman officials to post the crime of condemned criminals. Pilate affixed a sign in three languages—Greek, Hebrew and Latin—advertising the crime for which Jesus was convicted. At least one of these languages would have been understood by visitors to Jerusalem during the Passover celebrations. The purpose of the insignia was to warn potential criminals what their fate was destined to be should they be caught as Jesus was. *INRI* is an abbreviation for the Latin words *Iesus Nazarenus Rex Iudaeorum* meaning "Jesus the Nazarene, King of the Jews."

Occupations

Most Jews were farmers or herdsmen. They raised grapes, figs, fruits, olives and grain. They knew full well that God was the source of their crops, thus many of the great religious festivals were celebrations of thanksgiving for the products of the field. The people lived in villages and towns, but most of their employ-ment was in the open country where they won the necessities of life from the stony hillsides. Fishing was a major industry along the Sea of Galilee. Cities tended to be crowded but small. No one was much more than a quarter-mile from the open country.

Jesus himself was a carpenter. His customary work was to make everyday articles and tools like plows and yokes, winnow-ing forks and threshing sledges, tables and chairs and the like. He probably helped build houses, especially the doors and crossbeams.

Roman and Greek influence was strong in the Palestine of Jesus' day. For example, pious Jews gave their sons Greek names like Philip and Andrew. Roman coins, including those with the image of the emperor, were used even by those who fiercely hated Rome. For the most part, though, Jews believed they defiled themselves by associating with foreigners and prac-ticing their customs. The Jews were Yahweh's people and did not associate with others.

Synagogues were the only major buildings in all but the large cities. They were primarily prayer houses, although they were used for meeting places as well. Most private dwellings were made of stones from the fields put together with mud mixed with straw. There was very little lumber in Palestine. Tree trunks rested on the walls to help support flat roofs made of thatch and clay. Plumbing was almost unheard of.

The chief food of the poor was barley bread; only the rich made bread from wheat. Parched grain was common. Honey sweetened the food. Sheep and goat milk were more common than milk from cows. Eggs and meat were rare luxury items. Fish was the usual source of protein. Vegetables like broad beans, len-tils, cucumbers, onions and lettuce were plentiful. Boiled, powdered, candied or pickled locusts were considered a treat. Food was highly spiced. Many fruits and nuts supplemented the diet—grapes, dates, figs, melons, apricots, pomegranates, mulberries, walnuts, almonds and pistachios.

The rabbi (teacher) was the best-educated man in the community. He taught in the synagogue where a school was established for boys to memorize the Law and learn to read the scriptures. Ruling the village and ruling the synagogue were the same thing. Each synagogue elected a council of elders. They made local regulations and tried offenders in addition to conducting the religious services.

RELIGIOUS FEASTS

Research the meaning and practices of one of the following Jewish religious feasts:

- Passover
- Pentecost
- Feast of Trumpets
- Day of Atonement
- Feast of Tabernacles
- Feast of Dedication
- Purim

Women and Family Life

Jews respected women more than most peoples of the first century did, but by our standards they were still in a lowly position. Women were supposed to stay in the home. Rarely were they taught to read or to write. They had no official part in the synagogue and were only permitted to sit behind a screen or on a balcony. They were not expected to keep all the rules of the Torah (Law) because they were thought to be too weak to do so. Their heads were supposed to be covered in public places. In the home, though, the mother played a key role. In the worship service, for example, the mother lit the candle of joy thus beginning the Sabbath service.

Families were typically large, and children were considered a blessing. It was a curse to be childless. Boys were much more desirable than girls because they were the ones who cared for aging parents and carried on family traditions. Thus the Jewish law book, the Talmud, states: "The birth of a female child causes universal sorrow, whereas the birth of a male child causes universal joy." Finally, the parents usually arranged the marriages among their children.

JESUS AND WOMEN

What was Jesus' attitude toward women? Please read the following passages:

Luke 8:1-3 and Mark 15:40-41 (women follow him)

Matthew 19:1-9 (Jesus condemns divorce which men of his day could obtain with ease)

Luke 7:36-50 and John 4:1-42 (Jesus freely associates with women in public—a taboo in his day)

John 20:11-18 (Jesus appears first to a woman)

Discuss: What does Jesus' sensitivity to women reveal about him?

RELIGIOUS GROUPS IN JESUS' DAY

To get some picture of the religious ferment in our Lord's day, let us turn to a brief discussion of some of the religious groups around then. These are important in the total picture of Jesus' public ministry because representatives of some of them opposed Jesus' teaching and even conspired to put him to death.

Pharisees The Pharisees were the most important religious sect of Jesus' day. They are mentioned 99 times in the New Testament. Their name literally means "separated ones." Scholars are not sure of the derivation of this name. Some suggest that they "separated" themselves from the Maccabean revolt. Maybe it meant that the Pharisees separated themselves from the common people or perhaps from the Greeks and other non-Jews. Other scholars hold that it means they separated themselves from sin. These last two meanings are probably quite accurate because the Pharisees wanted very much to live lives

that would be especially pleasing to God so that he would send his Messiah to them.

Many of the scribes were Pharisees. (A *scribe* was a man trained in the Law; each sect had its scribes.) They added to the Law through their oral traditions which were collected in an important work known as the Talmud. These traditions gave detailed regulations about Sabbath observance, ceremonial washings and tithing.

Some of the Pharisees were the principal opponents of Jesus during his public ministry. He condemned some of their teachings and their hypocrisy. But some Pharisees were holy and included men like Gamaliel who had an open mind regarding the Christians:

> One member of the Sanhedrin, however, a Pharisee called Gamaliel, who was a doctor of the Law and respected by the whole people . . . addressed the Sanhedrin, "Men of Israel, be careful how you deal with these people. . . . If this enterprise, this movement of theirs, is of human origin it will break up of its own accord; but if it does in fact come from God you will not only be unable to destroy them, but you might find yourselves fighting against God" (Acts 5:34-39).

Many of the teachings and sayings of the Pharisees had value, but their extremely detailed interpretations of the Law burdened the average Jew with needless guilt and worry. The liberating gospel values of Jesus opposed these interpretations. The Pharisees who observed all the regulations sometimes fell into pride and looked down on all others.

A widely known convert to Christianity from the Pharisees was St. Paul.

Sadducees   While most of the Pharisees were laity, the bulk of the Sadducees came from priestly families, though a few wealthy and conservative lay people were in their numbers. They took their name from Sadok, a high priest in the time of Solomon.

In our Lord's day the Sadducees were the dominant party in

the Sanhedrin. They differed with the Pharisees on the following points:

- The Pharisees accepted both scripture and oral tradition; the Sadducees thought only the Torah (the Law) was revealed by God. (The Torah included the first five books of the Hebrew scriptures.)
- Because the Torah failed to mention it, the Sadducees rejected belief in the resurrection of the body. The Pharisees, like Jesus himself, taught the doctrine of bodily resurrection. For a similar reason, the Sadducees rejected belief in a final judgment and the existence of angels and devils. The Pharisees accepted these doctrines.
- The Sadducees were stricter than the Pharisees in applying the so-called *lex talionis* (the law of "an eye for an eye and a tooth for a tooth").
- The Pharisees emphasized God's control over human affairs whereas the Sadducees tended to stress human freedom.
- The Sadducees were sympathetic to Roman rule; the Pharisees despised the Romans and looked to the day when Yahweh would send a Messiah to free Israel.

The influence of the Sadducees waned and their numbers decreased after the destruction of the Jerusalem Temple in A.D. 70. From that time on the Pharisees enjoyed preeminence in the Jewish religion.

GAMALIEL

Read again Acts 5:34-39 (quoted on page 61. In your own words, what was Gamaliel's advice?

_____

_____

_____

_____

Discuss. As a class, come up with some examples of how Gamaliel's advice might apply even today.

Essenes   In 1948 a shepherd boy threw a rock into a cave and discovered what have become known as the Dead Sea scrolls. These belonged to the Essenes who hid them during the revolution against Rome that led to the destruction of the Temple in A.D. 70.

The Essenes are not mentioned in the New Testament. Josephus described them as a monastic community which practiced celibacy and held property in common. Many of them lived at Qumran, near where the Jordan River empties into the Dead Sea (see the map on page 54).

The Essenes strictly observed the Law but stayed away from the Temple and its official priesthood, which they did not acknowledge. They observed the Sabbath so strictly that they taught it was sinful to take care of basic bodily needs from sunup to sundown on that day.

They expected two messiahs, one who would be a king, the other a priest.

Jesus would have known of their existence, and some scholars maintain that John the Baptist might have known them quite well, perhaps at one time having been a member of their group. John baptized Jesus in the Jordan near the Qumran community.

Zealots   The Zealots were more political than religious, but it was not easy to separate the two in the Judaism of Jesus' day. Galilee served as their center of operations. They believed God would come to their aid if they took the initiative in throwing out the Roman oppressors. They were militaristic and could not tolerate the Romans. They believed that the coming messiah would be a great military leader who would throw off the yoke of the Romans. They would have looked on Jesus as a political messiah and most certainly were among those who wished to make Jesus a king. Their movement eventually led to the great revolt against Rome in A.D. 66-70.

Simon the Zealot was one of the apostles.

SUMMARY

1. The Jews had a profound sense of their history because they believed that God actively worked in it. He formed them as a people through Abraham, sustained them and gave them a land. Despite repeated Jewish infidelity to the covenant with Yahweh, God's love unerringly saw the Jewish people through some difficult times.

2. Jesus was a product of his Jewish heritage. He knew of God's special love for the Jews and his Father's saving intervention in the midst of persecution.

3. Palestine under Roman rule was once again ripe for Yahweh's saving intervention. Men like Herod the Great, Pilate and Herod Antipas made the Jews bitter and ever more desirous of a messiah who would deliver them from oppression.

4. Jesus traveled about the different sections of Palestine teaching the good news of salvation.

5. Jesus spoke Aramaic, a poetic language with some interesting stylistic devices.

6. Daily life in the Holy Land of our Lord's day revealed a difficult existence by our standards.

7. Groups like the Pharisees, Sadducees, Essenes and the Zealots all had different views on the proper religious response to God. Some of them perceived Jesus as a threat to their doctrines and established beliefs.

EXERCISES

1. Read several parables of Jesus, for example, the Mustard Seed (Mk 4:30-32), the Wily Manager (Lk 16:1-13), the Sower (Mt 13:4-23) and the Corrupt Judge (Lk 18:1-8). Identify points from the parables which reveal something about the social, agricultural and economic customs of Jesus' day.

2. Consult a bible atlas. Find Palestine in relationship to the Roman Empire's other provinces. In what way was Palestine in-

significant and yet very important? Why do you suppose this area has changed hands so many times during the course of history? Why is this area so important to today's history?

3. Visit a synagogue. Look for customs, practices and beliefs that give you an insight into Jesus' experience as a Jew. Note especially the Jews' profound respect for the Word of God as exemplified in their veneration of the Torah. Report to the class.

4. Visit a museum which exhibits clothing, housing and jewelry of our Lord's time, both from the Near East and from around the Roman Empire.

5. Prepare a meal based on the foods eaten in Jesus' day. You may want to consult a rabbi or ask Jewish friends to help you select foods that would be appropriate.

SCRIPTURE REFLECTION

Yahweh is my shepherd,
    I lack nothing.
In meadows of green grass he lets me lie.
To the waters of repose he leads me;
    there he revives my soul.
He guides me by paths of virtue
    for the sake of his name.
Though I pass through a gloomy valley,
    I fear no harm;
beside me your rod and your staff
    are there, to hearten me.
You prepare a table before me
    under the eyes of my enemies;
you anoint my head with oil,
    my cup brims over.
Ah, how goodness and kindness pursue me,
    every day of my life;
my home, the house of Yahweh,
    as long as I live! (Ps 23)

THREE

A Portrait
of the Human Jesus

The purposeful virility, the absolute genuineness, the austere uprightness, in a word the heroic in the personality of Jesus, is the first thing in his human character to strike the eye of the psychologist. It was this, too, which first bound the disciples to him.

—Karl Adam, *The Son of God*

Christians believe that Jesus is both true God and true man. This chapter will investigate the human Jesus, the Jesus who walked the dusty roads of Galilee, teaching, healing, being with others. We will take a smorgasbord sampling of the gospels to see what they reveal about the Jesus of history. We'll first reflect on what Jesus may have looked liked. Then we'll look at Jesus' sensitivity to others, his faithfulness as a friend, his ability as a teacher and his integrity. In Chapter 5 we will return once again to the gospels, but this time to see more systematically what each gospel writer had to say about Jesus.

Let's begin with the following exercise. First, imagine what Jesus was like when he walked the earth 20 centuries ago. Conjure up a vivid image of him—his physical appearance, the way he walked and talked, the way he dealt with people. Spend a few minutes with this mental picture of Jesus. Then respond to the statements below.

THE HUMAN JESUS

Directions: Mark each of the following *true* or *false*, then check your answers by reading the scripture passages given below.

____1. Like all humans, Jesus had to learn things throughout his childhood years.

____2. Jesus did not have any special friends.

____3. Jesus showed anger.

____4. Jesus never intended to begin a church.

____5. Jesus knew when the world was going to end.

____6. Jesus was against paying taxes.

____7. Jesus grew tired and thirsty.

____8. Jesus was like us in everything.

____9. Jesus rarely associated with women.

References:

1. Luke 2:52
2. John 21:20;11:3,35-36
3. Mark 11:15-19
4. Matthew 16:18
5. Mark 13:28-32
6. Mark 12:13-17
7. John 4:6;19:28
8. Hebrews 4:14-15
9. Luke 8:1-3

WHAT DID JESUS LOOK LIKE?

Christians through the ages have wondered what Jesus looked like. Two descriptions in particular vied for the attention of pious Christians in the very early centuries. The first was based on a prophecy from Second Isaiah which mentioned that the Suffering Servant of Yahweh would have a face people would scorn. Early Christians believed that the author of Second Isaiah was writing about Jesus. Thus church Fathers like Origen, Clement of Alexandria and Irenaeus characterized Jesus as small in stature, ill-favored and insignificant. They claimed he was without beauty, had a humble and mean appearance and looked like a slave. A very early tradition even claimed he was a leper.

A competing image emphasized Jesus' divine nature. Divinity and beauty were seen as qualities that went hand-in-hand. Thus the early tombs of Christians typically had flattering images of Jesus. To show that Jesus was greater than others, the artists of that day often depicted Jesus as taller than those to whom he was speaking. Church Fathers like John Chrysostom, Ambrose, Augustine and Jerome argued that Jesus was very handsome. They used the following scriptural passage to counteract the quotation from Second Isaiah:

> Of all men you are the most handsome,
> your lips are moist with grace,
> for God has blessed you for ever (Ps 45:2).

The battle over Jesus' physical appearance raged among early scholars and the pious for about five centuries, but eventually the artists won out. Almost all of them portrayed Jesus with a pleasing appearance. Of course, we can never adequately resolve the debate. The gospels do not tell us about Jesus' physical appearance. We do not have a first-century painting of him. Jews did not allow personal portraits because they condemned any image that might be worshiped.

In our day the debate over Jesus' appearance continues because of the scientific studies of the Shroud of Turin. This relic was brought to Italy by the crusaders in the 14th century. Many Christians believe it is the burial cloth which was used to wrap Jesus after he was taken down from the cross.

The latest scientific analyses seem to indicate that the Shroud of Turin is not a forgery. They do not, of course, prove that the cloth is a relic of Jesus, but they do indicate that the man who was wrapped in the Shroud had been scourged, crucified and lanced in the heart. He was bearded and wore long hair as was the custom for Jewish males in first-century Palestine. He might have been as much as 5 feet 10 inches tall. But the relic tells us little more about the physical appearance of the man wrapped in it. And again, no one can say with certitude if the Shroud is really the burial cloth of our Lord.

Many of us have a mental image of the human, historical Jesus. Much too often this image comes from pious art. Holy cards, for example, sometimes picture Jesus as a man with soft, effeminate features. Even though we do not have an authentic picture of Jesus, we can be confident that as a carpenter he must have been a muscular person with calloused hands. Further, we know that he was an outdoor person; he traveled up and down the countryside, trekked rocky roads and crossed hot desert sands. Jewish men who live in Israel today, especially those who work outdoors, have weathered faces with ruddy complexions, tanned by the sun. Jesus undoubtedly did too.

SOME EXERCISES

1. If you can draw, portray Jesus the way you imagine him to have been. As an alternative, write a short paragraph describing him. Describe the length of his hair, his beard, his eyes, his nose, his mouth, his smile, his voice, etc.

2. Read one of the new works out on the Shroud of Turin or the classic, *A Doctor at Calvary*, by Pierre Barbet. Make a report to the class.

3. St. Ignatius of Loyola, a great Christian mystic, taught that using our imaginations is an excellent aid to prayer. Do you have an image of Jesus when you pray to him? If so, does it help your prayer? Explain. Does it help to have a crucifix before you when you pray?

4. *Character of Jesus.* The gospels reveal little about the physical appearance of Jesus, but they tell us a lot about his character. Read the following passages and tell what you learn about Jesus' character:

   Mark 1:40-42: _____

   _____

   Luke 23:33-34: _____

   _____

   John 13:1-5: _____

   _____

   Matthew 15:32-39: _____

   _____

JESUS' SENSITIVITY

The gospels reveal that Jesus was a man of sensitivity. He responded to both the spoken and unspoken needs of the crowds who followed him. He could quiet fears, sometimes without ever uttering a word.

One of the most revealing scenes in all of the New Testament highlights the nonverbal communication of Jesus—Matthew's recounting of the Transfiguration. In Matthew 17:1-8 we see the majesty of a transfigured Jesus bedazzle a very confused and frightened Peter, James and John. When they heard the thunderous,

"This is my Son, the Beloved; he enjoys my favor.
Listen to him,"

they became extremely frightened and fell prostrate on the ground.

But Jesus came up and *touched* them. "Stand up,"
he said "do not be afraid." And when they raised
their eyes they saw no one but only Jesus (italics
added).

Of interest here is that Jesus *touched* them; we can only imagine the profound sense of peace that flowed through the apostles after their loving Master touched them.

Jesus touched many men, women and children during his all too brief ministry. Matthew also recounts how Jesus healed a repulsive leper by touching him and commanding him to be cured (Mt 8:1-4). John and Matthew both record how Jesus cured blind men after touching them.

But Luke tells one of the most memorable stories concerning Jesus' sensitivity to others (Lk 8:40-48). Jesus was going to the house of a man named Jairus. He was in a large crowd pressed by many people on all sides. A woman who had been bleeding for 12 years came up behind him and brushed against the tassel of his cloak. Her bleeding stopped immediately. But then Jesus asked, "Who touched me?" Imagine the dismay of Peter and his companions at this question. They made the obvious reply, "Master, it is the crowds round you, pushing."

Trembling, the woman finally came forth and admitted touching the Lord. She told the crowd what happened and how she had been cured instantly. Jesus dismissed her after saying that her faith had cured her. What is most interesting about this story is the way Jesus was aware of just one person in the midst of the many who were trying to get at him. He was sensitive to the *individual* person.

The nonverbal communication of Jesus displayed that he was "in touch" with people. Eye contact is another significant nonverbal cue mentioned in the New Testament to demonstrate how Jesus reached people. For example, imagine the deep love and forgiveness Jesus' eyes communicated to his chosen apostle Peter who had just denied knowing him for the third time. As Luke records, Peter was so moved with remorse that "he went outside and wept bitterly" (Lk 22:62). Not a word was spoken as Jesus' eyes met those of his friend. Through one glance, Jesus awakened in Peter profound repentance for his pitiful act of betrayal.

Jesus embodied loving concern for others. One of the most touching scenes in all the gospel concerns a sinning woman who broke into the house of Simon the Pharisee to anoint Jesus' feet and cry for forgiveness. The Pharisee thought ugly thoughts about her, condemning her and condemning Jesus for associating with her. But Jesus, who knew the agony of her soul, reached out, forgave her and told her to leave and sin no more.

This scene reminds us of his acceptance of the woman caught in adultery. Here was a known sinner caught in the act and brought before Jesus by the scribes and Pharisees. The Mosaic law prescribed death by stoning. But Jesus spoke up for her at the risk of further angering his enemies. Boldly he proclaimed,

"If there is one of you who has not sinned, let him
be the first to throw a stone at her" (Jn 8:7).

Then he began to write on the ground with his finger; his accusers shamefully turned away and withdrew. With tender love Jesus told her to be on her way, admonishing her to sin no more. His bold intervention had saved a life.

Too innumerable to list are the cures of the lame, blind, deaf and dumb, lepers, those tormented by mental afflictions and demon possession. In all of these the very human Jesus, who could and did suffer as we all do, identified with the suffering of others and reached out and freed them of their various infirmities.

Jesus was known as one who associated with all kinds of people. For example, it was taboo to go near a leper for fear of infection. Jesus not only went near lepers, but he overcame his own natural human revulsion to vile open sores and embraced these poor wretches. No respectable Jew would associate with the hated tax collectors who cooperated with the Roman occupation forces, but Jesus accepted dinner invitations from them and won some of them over, even numbering one of them as an apostle. It was also considered very bad manners for men to speak to women in public because of the fear of public scandal. Jesus not only spoke to women, but even spoke to one who was a hated Samaritan. Besides, women were among his closest followers, women like Mary and Martha and the reformed sinner, Mary of Magdala. Furthermore, Jesus went around with the poor, and this upset the rich. But he was also seen eating with the rich, for they were not excluded from his love. And most reprehensible of all to the established religious leaders of his day was his mingling with all kinds of sinners. He justified himself by saying,

> "It is not those who are well who need the doctor,
> but the sick" (Lk 5:31).

In summary, Jesus' sensitive compassion included everyone. His love excluded no one. His gentle healing touch, his glances of quiet understanding and kindness, his words of comfort and friendly encouragement, his merely being with people—all kinds of people, but especially the down-and-outers—all of these depict him as a strong man of good will and love. He was a true gentleman, a man sensitive to everyone's basic need to be accepted.

BEING SENSITIVE

1. It is not accidental that Jesus began his public ministry at about the age of 30. As Luke remarks, "Jesus increased in wisdom, in stature, and in favor with God and men" (Lk 2:52) before he was ready to proclaim the good news. Part of Jesus' education certainly was observing other people, becoming aware of their spoken and unspoken needs. The ability to read a person's suffering and deep personal hurts does not come easily. Those of us who wish to follow in our Lord's footsteps must practice observing people so that we can reach out to them and touch them with the same loving touch of Jesus our Lord. You may wish to try some of the following:

   • Take a close look at a classmate who does not seem to fit in. In what way does the person reveal his or her loneliness? Is it in the nervous tapping of fingers on the desk or in an inability to meet your eyes or in a nervous moving around? This classmate may well be nonverbally communicating the need for a friend, someone to talk to, someone to recognize him or her. Perhaps your sensitivity to these nonverbal cues will prompt you to go out of your way to speak with this person.

   • Get on a crowded bus. Look at the old people, especially those forced to stand while younger people sit. Note the way the "sitters" avoid eye contact with the people who are standing. They are nonverbally stating that they do not wish to recognize the existence of the others. Perhaps you will be aware of this situation the next time you are seated and the bus becomes crowded.

   • How do your parents, brothers, sisters and friends communicate nonverbally that they are tired and irritable? Pacing, fidgeting, nervous tapping and the like? Perhaps an understanding word on your part, a touch or an embrace, can help in such a situation. Report on the results of any of these experiments in human love.

2. *Needing love.* Read the following scriptural passages and respond to the exercises below.

   > My dear people,
   > let us love one another
   > since love comes from God
   > and everyone who loves is begotten by God and
   >   knows God (1 Jn 4:7).

"I give you a new commandment:
love one another;
just as I have loved you,
you also must love one another.
By this love you have for one another,
everyone will know that you are my disciples"
    (Jn 13:34-35).

By "love" here, Jesus means:

_____ a. action—giving myself to others

_____ b. attitude—finding the best in others

_____ c. seeking out others and demonstrating sensitivity toward them

_____ d. all of these

_____ e. (add your own)_____

Rewrite these scriptural passages in a way that says exactly what they mean for you. Use real examples.

Sample:

"I give you a new commandment:
You must share your time with a lonely classmate,
just as I shared my life with you. . . ."

JESUS AND FRIENDSHIP

Friendship enables us to bridge the loneliness of our existence. In and through friendship we find a reason to live as well as a reason to die. All of us, young and old alike, need and value friends.

What is friendship? Friendship is a kind of love. It is more than sharing a Coke on a hot day or working together on a difficult homework assignment. It is the sharing of a life. The Greeks used the term *philia,* "friendship-love," to distinguish it from other kinds of love.

The scriptures show that Jesus had some deep friendships. For example, on several occasions John the apostle is called "beloved" or "the disciple Jesus loved." As he hung dying on the cross, Jesus entrusted the care of his mother Mary to his close friend John:

> Seeing his mother and the disciple he loved standing near her, Jesus said to his mother, "Woman, this is your son." Then to the disciple he said, "This is your mother." And from that moment the disciple made a place for her in his home (Jn 19:26-27).

Certainly Jesus treated John as a close brother when he called him the son of Mary.

One of the most moving portraits of Jesus involving friendship concerns his relationship to Lazarus. Try to picture the scene. Jesus was away from Bethany, the home of Lazarus and his sisters, Mary and Martha. When he received word that his friend was dying, he postponed coming despite his great love for Lazarus. Finally Jesus announced to his apostles that it was time to go to Bethany, even though the apostles greatly feared that Jesus would be arrested by the authorities there and be put to death. Bethany was only two miles from Jerusalem.

When Jesus arrived, he was informed that Lazarus had already died and that his corpse lay rotting in the tomb for four days. Martha came to greet him and in her impetuous way rather strongly pointed out to Jesus, "If you had been here, my brother would not have died." Her thoughts must have included the idea that though Jesus had cured many sick people he had neglected one of his closest friends in his final hours of life. Her sister Mary echoed that thought when she too cried out, "Lord, if you had been here, my brother would not have died." Continuing from John's narrative:

> At the sight of her tears, and those of the Jews who followed her, Jesus said in great distress, with a sigh that came straight from the heart, "Where have you put him?" They said, "Lord, come and see." Jesus wept; and the Jews said, "See how much he loved him!" (Jn 11:33-36).

Jesus then brought his friend Lazarus back to life. Here is a picture of great human friendship, loyalty and love. It depicts not a "holy card Jesus" but a real man with real emotions.

LAZARUS

Please read John 11. Why did Jesus delay in coming to Lazarus? What important lesson did he teach by this miracle?

Our Friendship With Jesus

In discussing Jesus as a friend, we cannot neglect his relationship to us as friends. Again, it is John's gospel that underscores this theme. Read some of the most important words spoken by Jesus in his earthly ministry:

> "You are my friends,
> if you do what I command you.
> I shall not call you servants any more,
> because a servant does not know
> his master's business;
> I call you friends,
> because I have made known to you
> everything I have learnt from my Father.
> You did not choose me,
> no, I chose you;
> and I commissioned you
> to go out and to bear fruit" (Jn 15:14-16).

What power there is behind the statement, "You are my friends"! In Jesus' eyes we are no longer slaves nor mere creatures. We are his friends. What is the meaning of this incredible statement? For one thing, a friend is a very special person whom we cherish for what he or she is. A friend is someone we love unconditionally. A friend is that "someone other" who makes our life more meaningful.

To drive this point home a bit more, please think of your best friend. Have you ever considered why this person of all the hundreds of people you have met is your very best friend? It is a mystery. Very few of us could state exactly why the person we are thinking about now is our best friend. We Christians believe that God's love shines through our friends. The Lord sends them into our lives to enrich us and to bring us happiness. We do not think friends come into our lives as the result of pure chance.

Psychologist-priest Ignace Lepp wrote that our best friend is the special person in our life because he or she represents the ideal person we wish to be. That person has some quality which we so wish to emulate that we befriend that person in order to become like him or her. And this, according to Lepp, most often happens unconsciously or subconsciously.

This, however, is only half the story. Our friend sees something in us, too. Friendship is reciprocal; it works both ways. Our friends, in other words, cherish us because they see something valuable, something worthwhile, something they wish to emulate in us. In a real way, what happens to us happens to our friend. If we grow, our friend grows. And vice versa.

Jesus probably understood friendship in terms similar to this. We can clearly see why we would want to call Jesus our friend. Here is God's Son, the perfect human being, the man of truth, of conviction, of obedience unto death. Here is the perfect teacher understanding, patient and kind. Here is the perfect lover, the one willing to give even his life that his friends might have superabundant life. Any reasonable person would want to have Jesus as a friend.

John's gospel emphatically states that Jesus calls us his

friends. Ponder that truth and what it implies. He sees in us something so worthwhile that he was willing to die for us. He so loves us that he calls us friends. And he continually calls us friends. Our Christian belief maintains that we merely have to accept his invitation to friendship. Part of his message is that no matter what we do throughout our lives, no matter how we go astray, we should always remember the call of his friendship: "I call you friends." Despair and ill-feeling toward ourselves should never lead us to reject this invitation. We are so valuable in our Lord's eyes that he calls us friends!

FRIENDSHIP

1. Read the following passages and briefly describe the quality of friendship shown:

   Mark 1:29-31 _____

   _____

   Luke 11:5-8 _____

   _____

   Matthew 18:21-22 _____

   _____

   Luke 23:39-43 _____

   _____

   John 20:24-29 _____

   _____

2. The following traits typify good friendships. Rate yourself according to your relationship with your best friend and with Jesus.

   4—describes me very well
   3—describes me most of the time
   2—describes me some of the time
   1—I'm weak on this one

	Friend	Jesus
a. I spend time with my friend/Jesus.	_____	_____
b. I listen to my friend/Jesus.	_____	_____
c. I admire my friend/Jesus.	_____	_____
d. I accept my friend/Jesus.	_____	_____
e. I love my friend/Jesus.	_____	_____
f. I give to my friend/Jesus.	_____	_____

g. I gracefully receive from
my friend/Jesus. _____ _____

h. I am totally honest with my
friend/Jesus. _____ _____

i. I am not afraid to tell
others about my friendship. _____ _____

Add to this list.

j. _____ _____ _____

k. _____ _____ _____

Discuss: As a class talk about how we can exhibit each of the
traits listed above in our friendship with Jesus.

3. Discuss the following:

a. What is involved in having someone be your friend? What
kind of obligations does it place on you? In what way does
it make you more free?

b. Do you agree that your friend is someone you wish to be
like? If so, in what way? If not, why not?

What is most lovable in you?_____

_____

What would a close friend say?_____

_____

What would the Lord say?_____

_____

c. Do young people today have a hard time accepting the
weeping Jesus described at the tomb of Lazarus? Do
adults? Discuss some of the factors in contemporary
society which force men to put on a stoic face in the type
of situation described in John's gospel. Is this changing?
Ask your parents to respond to these questions.

JESUS AS TEACHER

Jesus was an effective teacher. He spoke in terms which his audience could easily relate to and understand. For example, his teaching reveals a person very much in touch with nature. In his famous Sermon on the Mount he leaves us an image of mental and psychological health few modern psychiatrists could improve. Consider his words:

> "That is why I am telling you not to worry about your life and what you are to eat, nor about your body and how you are to clothe it. Surely life means more than food, and the body more than clothing! Look at the birds in the sky. They do not sow or reap or gather into barns; yet your heavenly Father feeds them. Are you not worth much more than they are? Can any of you, for all his worrying, add one single cubit to his span of life? And why worry about clothing? Think of the flowers growing in the fields; they never have to work or spin; yet I assure you that not even Solomon in all his regalia was robed like one of these" (Mt 6:25-29).

By using beautiful images from nature, Jesus was instructing his followers that today has worries enough of its own. If we take care of the important matters of life, the less important will take care of themselves. Our absolute faith in the loving Father should be like that of trusting children. When we surrender ourselves to God we are led to inner peace and calmness which are fundamental to emotional and mental health.

As we have seen in the last chapter, Jesus' audience was close to the natural world. As a result, his followers and close disciples would have easily grasped the similes he used to explain the kingdom of God. For example, the minuteness of the mustard seed and its sure growth into a bushy tree could easily be pictured by the Jews of Jesus' day. A people who made their own bread certainly could not miss the inevitability of the spread of God's kingdom when likened to yeast. Parables of vineyards, tenant farmers and straying sheep easily resonated in the experience of an agricultural and pastoral people.

Jesus possessed an imaginative mind which expressed a sense of awe and mystery in the wonders of natural phenomena, as witnessed by the following quotation:

> "The wind blows wherever it pleases;
> you hear its sound,
> but you cannot tell where it comes from or where
> it is going.
> That is how it is with all who are born of the Spirit"
> (Jn 3:8).

Jesus was a teacher who related to people on their level. He did not wait for them to come to him; he went to them. He was a wandering preacher who taught everywhere—on hillsides, at the dinner tables of both rich and poor, on dusty roads, in synagogues and in the Temple—wherever people were willing to hear the Good News.

Jesus' language was concrete and to the point. Instead of saying, "Charity should not be ostentatious," Jesus said,

> "So when you give alms, do not have it trumpeted before you; this is what the hypocrites do in the synagogues and in the streets to win men's admiration. I tell you solemnly, they have had their reward" (Mt 6:2).

Again, Jesus could have said, "Hypocritical prejudice is unbecoming," but he chose instead to paint an almost humorous example by stating:

> "Why do you observe the splinter in your brother's eye and never notice the plank in your own? How dare you say to your brother, 'Let me take the splinter out of your eye,' when all the time there is a plank in your own? Hypocrite! Take the plank out of your own eye first, and then you will see clearly enough to take the splinter out of your brother's eye" (Mt 7:3-5).

Even today we can relate to this kind of language. Jesus' parables exude a kind of earthiness. Jesus was not a prude. He noticed and enjoyed material things. He changed water into wine not only to teach that faith brings about a tremendous transformation, but to help a married couple celebrate their wedding day.

His enemies accused him of being a glutton, of eating and drinking with all kinds of people. He was not enough of a "stick-in-the-mud" for them. He was too earthy, too concrete.

Perhaps more than the language he used, the way he taught upset his enemies. He taught on his own authority. He quoted no other teacher. When other rabbis taught, they quoted other rabbis (that is, their teachers). Jesus did not, and yet he enjoyed tremendous popularity with the people. This disturbed the official scribes, the Pharisees and the Sadducees. Their continual lament was "Where did he get all of this?" As a result, they were bent on tricking Jesus, trying to get him to slip up and make a ridiculous statement. There are numerous examples in the New Testament where Jesus is called on to debate with his opponents in defense of both himself and his teaching. It is in these conflict situations that Jesus shines as a teacher.

Two examples will help illustrate Jesus' ability to confront his opponents. The first concerns our Lord's answer to the Sadducees' question concerning the resurrection of the body. The Sadducees did not believe in this doctrine because they claimed it could not be found in the Torah, the only part of the Old Testament they thought was authoritative. So they posed the ridiculous case of a woman who successively married seven brothers because each died before leaving her with a child. (Under Mosaic law, a brother had to marry his brother's widow if no children had resulted from the marriage.) They coyly asked, "Now, at the resurrection, to which of them will she be wife since she had been married to all seven?" Jesus saw through their insincerity. However, he gave them the benefit of the doubt when he responded:

> "The children of this world take wives and husbands, but those who are judged worthy of a place in the other world and in the resurrection from the dead do not marry because they can no longer die, for they are the same as the angels, and being children of the resurrection they are sons of God" (Lk 20:34-36).

Jesus' real cleverness, though, rests in his quotation of the Torah to show the stiff-necked Sadducees that there *are* references to the resurrection:

"And Moses himself implies that the dead rise again, in the passage about the bush where he calls the Lord *the God of Abraham, the God of Isaac and the God of Jacob.* Now he is God, not of the dead, but of the living; for to him all men are in fact alive" (Lk 20:37-38).

Jesus thus stated that Moses (authorship of the Torah was attributed to him) taught the doctrine of the resurrection. He did this by arguing that Moses would not have referred to Abraham, Isaac and Jacob in the present tense unless he believed they were alive with God. Jesus knew his scriptures better than his opponents. They walked away afraid to ask him anything else.

A second example involves the coin of tribute offered Jesus by the Pharisees. Their question was designed to catch Jesus in a seditious statement so that he could be turned over to the Romans for advocating revolution. His response was the brilliant statement,

"Very well, give back to Caesar what belongs to Caesar—and to God what belongs to God" (Mt 22:21).

He refused to be trapped in their games and turned them away shaking their heads in dismay.

One final comment about Jesus the teacher: He had the uncanny ability to stretch people's minds. He led them on to deeper understandings and more sensitive awarenesses. He did this by effective use of paradox. A paradox is an apparent contradiction. It is a figure of speech which takes thought. Jesus used a number of these that Christians have pondered for ages. Study the following paradox:

"Yes, it is easier for a camel to pass through the eye of a needle than for a rich man to enter the kingdom of God" (Lk 18:25).

Apparently, this saying paints a very dim picture for the rich. A camel cannot pass through the eye of a needle and, by comparison, a rich man cannot be saved. But as Jesus responded to the shock of his listeners' questions about who can be saved:

"Things that are impossible for men" he replied
"are possible for God" (Lk 18:27).

What Jesus warns against is a person attempting to earn or
merit entrance into God's kingdom. Salvation can be accomplished only through a miracle of God's grace accepted in
humility and faith. The rich man errs if he trusts in his riches to
buy him salvation. Jesus does not mean to say that a rich person
cannot be saved. What he is stressing is that persons who have
material possessions in abundance are tempted to be so blinded
by them that they might fail to see the kingdom of God irrupting
into the world when they are called to accept Jesus in faith.

JESUS THE TEACHER

1. As a class, list at least 10 traits of an ideal teacher. How does Jesus fit your description?

2. *Paradox.* Here are several paradoxes and riddles from the teachings of Jesus. First try to figure out what each means. Write an interpretation in the space provided. Then, discuss as a class your individual interpretations. Verify your findings by consulting a bible commentary on Luke's gospel.

   a. "For anyone who wants to save his life will lose it; but anyone who loses his life for my sake, that man will save it" (Lk 9:24).

   _____

   b. "For the least among you all, that is the one who is great" (Lk 9:48b).

   _____

   c. "For everyone who exalts himself will be humbled, and the man who humbles himself will be exalted" (Lk 14:11).

   _____

   d. "I tell you, of all the children born of women, there is no one greater than John; yet the least in the kingdom of God is greater than he is" (Lk 7:28).

   _____

   e. "I have come to bring fire to the earth, and how I wish it were blazing already!" (Lk 12:49).

   _____

   Discuss: What is the major problem with this quote? Can you find one that seems to contradict it?

3. Read the following passages and note how Jesus manifested his debating ability:

   Matthew 21:23-27 —the authority of Jesus

   Mark 7:1-23 —the question of tradition and intent of the commandments

   Mark 12:35-37 —the son and Lord of David (in reference to the Messiah)

   Luke 20:9-19 —Parable of the Tenants

THE INTEGRITY OF JESUS

We dislike phonies. The do-as-I-say-not-as-I-do mentality of so many people in our modern world turns us off. Hypocrisy disgusts us. It was as much a problem in Jesus' day as it is today. For example, Jesus' opponents seemed to be victim to it. They often asked others to do what they themselves would not do, or they performed their religious duties just so others would think well of them. Jesus used some very strong language in rebuking these hypocrites, calling them "fools," "blind guides," "whitewashed tombs," "serpents" and "brood of vipers." It took a strong man to speak like this—a genuine and honest man, one totally opposite to what he condemned.

Jesus was a genuine person. He did not merely rail against the phoniness of those religious guides who bound the consciences of others. He himself translated into deed what he proclaimed in word. He was the epitome of an honest man: He lived what he taught.

What is it that Jesus said that was so opposed to the teaching and way of life of the hypocrites with whom he came in contact? The Sermon on the Mount provides an answer. It teaches the value of inner disposition. Jesus calls his followers to be light, to be transparent, to be authentic witnesses of the gospel. Christians are called to pray, give alms to the poor and fast in loving and humble ways, not to build up an image in front of others. God knows the good deeds we do.

Jesus' preaching calls us to love even our enemies. We should do good to those who hate us. This is the test of genuine love of God: Can we love even our enemy? This kind of love demands that we forgive. Genuine love is forgiving love. Jesus wanted to reveal that God is forgiving love. We imitate God's love by extending his forgiveness to others.

Jesus' message was one he lived. He backed up his words with actions. He not only taught that we should forgive 70 times seven, but he himself forgave all kinds of people. He even forgave those who put him to death:

> "Father, forgive them; they do not know what they
> are doing" (Lk 23:34).

Jesus lived the love he preached by dying for us. His passion and his death are the greatest testimony to his genuineness. We notice people who back up their words with action. We notice Jesus because he freely gave his life for us. He lived the message of love that he preached. His death on the cross for us proves it. (We will examine the actual passion and crucifixion and its meaning for us in Chapter 6.)

REFLECTION

1. Who is the most genuine person you know?

   _____

2. What makes this person this way?_____

   _____

   _____

3. Which of the following traits do young people most admire in another person? Rank these traits from *1*, most admired, to *6*, least admired.

   ____genuineness   ____humility

   ____gentleness   ____industriousness

   ____intelligence   ____courage

   Which traits above would you like to be known for?

   _____

   Why? _____

   _____

4. Do you admire Jesus Christ? Why or why not?

Share your responses to these questions with at least one other person.

SUMMARY

1. Many people find it helpful to have a mental image of Jesus when they pray to him. Unfortunately, there is no evidence from the first century to tell us what Jesus looked like. He certainly would have had the features of a Jew and the appearance of one who labored as a carpenter and spent much time outdoors.

2. The gospels do present a psychological portrait of Jesus. For example, they reveal that Jesus was a man of profound sensitivity. He associated with all kinds of people, cured their ailments, and knew how to relate to them as individuals with dignity and worth.

3. The gospels tell us that Jesus was a loyal friend. He calls us his friends, too. This special love he has for us is one of the most powerful truths God has ever revealed to us.

4. Jesus was also an outstanding teacher. His teaching was down-to-earth and challenged people to think and exercise their imaginations. He was also an excellent debater when challenged by his enemies.

5. Jesus was a totally honest, genuine man who lived the message of forgiving love that he taught. His death showed that he practiced what he preached.

EXERCISE

We Christians believe that Jesus is the mediator between God and us. We believe that the human person of Jesus reveals God. For example, by seeing the human Jesus the apostles were actually seeing the Father. By getting to know Jesus' human character we get to know something about God's revelation.

This exercise is designed for you to learn something more about Jesus, so that you can get to know something about how God has revealed himself to us.

Directions:

1. Divide into six groups. Read the following chapters of Mark's gospel:

   Group 1: Mark 1-2   Group 4: Mark 7-8
   Group 2: Mark 3-4   Group 5: Mark 9-10
   Group 3: Mark 5-6   Group 6: Mark 11-12

2. In your reading, focus on the *words* of Jesus and his *actions.* Find at least 10 examples that tell you something about his character.

3. As a group, compose a paragraph describing the Jesus whom you discovered in these chapters of Mark. Use what was discussed in this chapter as a guide.

4. Share your "portraits" of Jesus with the rest of the class.

5. Discuss as a class what this human Jesus (the portraits you composed) tells us about God.

SCRIPTURE REFLECTION

. . . but there is nothing meritorious in taking a beating patiently if you have done something wrong to deserve it. The merit, in the sight of God, is in bearing it patiently when you are punished after doing your duty.

This, in fact, is what you were called to do, because Christ suffered for you and left an example for you to follow the way he took. He had not done anything wrong, and *there had been no perjury in his mouth.* He was insulted and did not retaliate with insults; when he was tortured he made no threats but he put his trust in the righteous judge. He was *bearing our faults* in his own body on the cross, so that we might die to our faults and live for holiness; *through his wounds you have been healed.* You had *gone astray like sheep* but now you have come back to the shepherd and guardian of your souls (1 Pt 2:20-25).

FOUR

The Message of Jesus

He is a path, if any be misled;
He is a robe, if any naked be;
If any chance to hunger, he is bread;
If any be a bondman, he is free;
If any be but weak, how strong is he!
To dead men life he is, to sick men health;
To blind men sight, and to the needy wealth;
A pleasure without loss, a treasure without stealth.
—Giles Fletcher

This chapter will present some basic teachings of Jesus. He taught in both words and deeds, and his parables were vivid picture-stories that helped his *spoken* message come alive for his audience. They continue to teach the good news even to those of us living in the last decades of the 20th century. His miracles were striking demonstrations of God's power and important signs of God's love working through our Lord Jesus. As *actions,* they also communicate vital truths about the kingdom of God and Jesus who came to proclaim it.

This chapter will look at the message of Jesus as he proclaimed it in word and deed. We will look especially to his parables and miracles to see how they reveal the Lord's good news of God's love for us.

HEARING THE GOOD NEWS OF JESUS

Before discussing Jesus' message, please examine your beliefs on the following points concerning the good news of Jesus. Mark according to this scale:

4 — I strongly believe this
3 — I believe this
2 — I am uncertain on this point
1 — I don't believe this

_____ 1. There are some areas in my life that need work and improvement.

_____ 2. I am a sinner in need of our Lord's healing touch.

_____ 3. I know that God loves me beyond my wildest imaginings.

_____ 4. The Lord has forgiven my sins.

_____ 5. My basic obligation in life is to love God above all things and show that love by responding to the needs of others.

_____ 6. Deep down I guess I'd say that I am a joyful person.

_____ 7. If I *really* believed what Jesus taught, I would change the way I am.

_____ 8. Miracles can happen even today.

_____ 9. Some people claim that Christianity has been a failure; maybe that's because not enough people have truly tried to live it.

_____10. Jesus Christ is my personal savior and the savior of the world who calls on us to care for one another.

Discuss: Share your responses to items 8 and 9 above. Begin by defining the term *miracle*.

Personal Reflection. Write a short essay explaining your response to item 1 or 7 above. Share your essay with a friend if you care to.

There are as many summaries of the teachings of Jesus as there are scholars who address themselves to the topic. We now turn to a summary by Father Andrew Greeley which contains the essential teaching of the Lord during his earthly ministry. We shall discuss each point in turn.

1. God's kingdom is here. We are called to change the way we are living, to accept the good news.

2. Salvation is taking place right now.

3. God is our loving father, our Abba. The key sign that the kingdom is here and that salvation is happening is that our Abba loves us and forgives us.

4. The kingdom will triumph despite all opposition to it.

5. As disciples of the Lord, those who have accepted the good news, we must live joyfully.

GOD'S KINGDOM IS HERE . . . CHANGE . . . ACCEPT THE GOOD NEWS

The clearest and most succinct statement of Jesus' preaching appears in the opening verses of Mark's gospel:

> "The time has come" he said "and the kingdom of God is close at hand. Repent, and believe the Good News" (Mk 1:15).

In contrast to Mark's expression "kingdom of God," Matthew uses the expression "kingdom of heaven." The author of Matthew's gospel, writing for a Jewish-Christian audience which held Yahweh's name in high esteem, wished to avoid mentioning the sacred name. But the idea behind "kingdom of God" and "kingdom of heaven" is the same.

Meaning of "Kingdom of God"   The phrase "kingdom of God" was not original with Jesus. Both Old Testament writers and rabbis who taught in Jesus' day used it.

The expression has its roots in the early political history of Israel. The Chosen People had become dissatisfied with their rulers and petitioned Yahweh to give them a king who would rule with Yahweh's justice, unlike the earthly justice of the Canaanite kings. The Jews believed that Yahweh created and sustained the Jewish nation, so he should be the real ruler in Israel; they begged for a king to represent their true heavenly ruler. The problem with Israel's kings, though, was that they proved to be self-serving; their kingdoms also tended to be oppressive. King David was the very best of Israel's kings, but even he had his shortcomings.

Around David's time the belief and promise emerged that one day a son of David would rule with Yahweh's justice. The promised one would bring Yahweh's peace to the land, justice to the poor, and comfort to widows and orphans. Because of the promise that the day of the Lord's rule would eventually come, rabbis of Jesus' day taught the people that they ought to live as though the kingdom or reign of God had actually come. They knew quite well that God's kingdom was not yet established, but they thought that if people started to live a life that was ruled by Law, they would find their relationships with others changing. These rabbis taught that God's spirit would live in their fellow Jews if people acted as though the kingdom had indeed come.

What was unique about Jesus' teaching concerning the kingdom was his announcement that the kingdom had indeed arrived. The signs were all around. He himself figured prominently in the announcement that the kingdom of God is here; for example, in Luke's gospel, we see Jesus reading at a synagogue service from a passage in Isaiah that foretold what would happen when God's reign became established:

> The spirit of the Lord has been given to me,
> for he has anointed me.
> He has sent me to bring the good news to the poor,
> to proclaim liberty to captives
> and to the blind new sight,
> to set the downtrodden free,
> to proclaim the Lord's year of favor (Lk 4:18-19).

As Jesus returned to his seat, all in the synagogue had their eyes on him. They were transfixed by his dramatic reading and were awaiting anxiously some further word from him. Jesus slowly turned, looked at all of them and said:

> "This text is being fulfilled today even as you listen."

Today, in other words, Yahweh's kingdom has come, great things are taking place. And this is happening right now before your very eyes.

Meaning of "Repent"   Because God's kingdom is actively present in the world, Jesus preached that we should do something about it. First, we should repent, that is, change our lives. And then we should believe the good news that God's kingdom is here now, working in our midst.

The English word *repent* (in the Greek *metanoia*) means "change your heart," that is, change the way you are doing things. Why does the announcement of God's kingdom call for a change in heart? The answer is simple—Jesus is here, so reality and what life is all about are now radically different. Before, we were living selfishly and bitterly toward our neighbor, neglecting both our God and others. But now reality is excitingly different. God and his peace and his justice and his Son have broken into human history. The task now is to get back on the right track. The job is to wake up and change our ways and readily accept the new order of things. We show that we accept the new order of things by loving God above all things and our neighbor as ourselves.

Metanoia conjures up the picture of a person on a road who is going in the wrong direction, a person who is lost. Jesus enters the picture. He announces that God's reign of peace and love has broken into human history. We should wake up and see the light! We should turn around and change the way we are doing things. We get into the kingdom of God by believing in it and accepting it. The sign that we accept it is by living a love-filled life which takes into consideration other people, not just ourselves.

THE KINGDOM AND YOU

Has God's kingdom touched your heart? Are you changing your life—a lifelong task—so that God's love, peace and justice can reign in your heart? Please rate yourself on the following attitudes and practices.

4 — This has top priority in my life right now

3 — I'm making good progress on this

2 — I'm having some success on this, but some setbacks, too

1 — I need plenty of work on this

_____1. I'm rooting out those things in my life which tend to blind me to God and others, for example, dependence on drugs, material possessions, what others think of me.

_____2. I make an effort to see God's work in the world today, for example, the love he has for me personally.

_____3. I am helping to further God's kingdom by giving some of my time and talents to others in need.

_____4. I spend some time each day in prayer asking our Lord to show me how I can love him and others more.

_____5. I genuinely believe the good news that God is actively at work both in the world and in my life.

Discuss:

1. How does God work in the world today?
2. Does he work through you? Explain.

SALVATION IS TAKING PLACE RIGHT NOW

Jesus used a number of poetic images to announce that the day of the Lord had come. Among them are the following: the good shepherd gathering together the lost sheep; the father of a family calling his family around him and inviting guests to dinner; a physician coming to heal the sick; a king sending a messenger with invitations to a wedding feast; an architect building a new temple while a king makes a triumphal entry. Each of these images, along with images of new wine being poured into new wineskins, a time of new harvest and new vintage, a time to put on new robes—all of these announce rather vividly that the new age of God's kingdom has been ushered in.

This new age is a time of salvation. We Christians believe that Jesus is our Savior, that he has brought us salvation. But what is the meaning of this? A derivative of the English word *salvation* hints at the New Testament understanding of the word. *Salve* is "a cream or lotion put on a sore or wound to heal it." *Salvation* means "healing"; Jesus the Savior brings healing and salvation to us as he ushers in the day of the Lord. This particular interpretation of the word is very clear in the gospel scene where John the Baptist sent messengers to Jesus to ask him if he is the Promised One. Jesus did not give John's emissaries a direct yes or no; rather, he loosely quoted Isaiah:

> "Go back and tell John what you have seen and heard: the blind see again, the lame walk, lepers are cleansed, and the deaf hear, the dead are raised to life, the Good News is proclaimed to the poor and happy is the man who does not lose faith in me" (Lk 7:22-23).

For Jesus, salvation consists in making whole again, in healing our wounds, the gaping wounds that separate us from God and from our fellow humans. As the Son of God, the agent of the Father, Jesus came to cure the festering psychological and spiritual wounds that cause people to hate and reject themselves and others, and to help alleviate the physical suffering due to illness, birth defects, old age and the like.

God's salvation and healing come through Jesus. His power to overcome our spiritual, psychological and physical sicknesses has broken into the world. The miracles of Jesus are the sign of God's power.

Miracles of Jesus   What is a miracle? The modern mind understands *miracle* as "a suspension of the laws of nature." The problem with this understanding of miracle is that once we discover particular laws in nature which explain what we once thought were miracles, we tend to stop believing in miracles.

But the New Testament has a religious understanding of miracle. In the synoptic gospels the Greek word *dynamis* is used for "miracle"; in John's gospel, the word *semeion* is used. *Dynamis* (compare the English words *dynamic* and *dynamite*) means "power." Thus, when the gospels of Matthew, Mark and Luke record a miracle of Jesus, they are trying to show that God's power has broken into human history to overcome the forces of darkness and to heal the wounds of the world.

Semeion means "sign"; hence St. John's gospel treats the miracles of Jesus as profound signs of deeper realities. He records seven signs, one of them being the raising of Lazarus from the dead. Besides demonstrating that the power of God can overcome even death, the raising of Lazarus is a powerful sign that it is through Jesus that our own resurrection takes place. The ultimate salvation—the overpowering of the terrible sickness of death—comes through Jesus. He is the resurrection and the life. We are dead without him.

Jesus performed miracles, then, as a way to preach about God's kingdom and its salvation. They were visible signs of God's power which helped demonstrate the mission of Jesus, revealed his identity as the Savior and Messiah, and showed him to be God.

The miracles show that Jesus' mission is to make people whole, to show them that God is working in their midst.

The miracles reveal Jesus as the one who was promised in the Old Testament. He is the promised Messiah who accomplishes great deeds of liberation, of salvation, especially for the poor and the lowly.

The miracles also reveal that Jesus is God himself. He who sees Jesus sees the Father. After Jesus cures the paralytic in John's gospel, he says:

> "Thus, as the Father raises the dead and gives
> them life,
> so the Son gives life to anyone he chooses;
>
> For the Father, who is the source of life,
> has made the Son the source of life" (Jn 5:21,26).

MIRACLES OF JESUS

Scholars have divided the miracles of Jesus into three broad categories: healing miracles, exorcisms (chasing out evil demons), and nature miracles. Below is a list of some of the principal miracles of Jesus in each of these categories.

1. Please read one version of each miracle. Note what has taken place on the surface level; for example, Jesus cures a man's blindness.

2. Discuss the meaning of the miracle. In other words, how does this miracle proclaim God's kingdom, his salvation, his good news in the person of Jesus? In the example of the blind man you might say that his faith in Jesus enabled him to see that God works through his son Jesus who enables us to walk in the light.

3. With your classmates compare and contrast the various versions of the miracles you have studied.

	Matthew	*Mark*	*Luke*	*John*
Healing Miracles				
The blind man (men) of Jericho	20:29-34	10:46-52	18:35-43	
The leper in Capernaum	8:2-4	1:40-45	5:12-14	
Malchus			22:49-51	18:10-11
Exorcisms				
The demoniac		1:23-28	4:33-37	
Possessed mute	9:32-34			
Nature Miracles				
Multiplying bread	14:15-21	6:30-44	9:10-17	6:1-15
Calming the storm	8:23-27	4:35-41	8:22-25	
The catch of fish			5:1-11	

GOD IS OUR LOVING FATHER . . .

At the very heart of Jesus' good news is his message of the love and mercy of his Father. Although our God loves us as a father loves a child, his love goes far beyond any human standard. His love for us is incredibly generous!

Three of Jesus' parables drive home the message of God's loving mercy particularly well. They are known as the three "lost" parables. They are among the most familiar parables, but their very familiarity often makes us take their simple message for granted.

Please pause here and read these three parables—the Lost Coin, the Lost Sheep and the Lost (Prodigal) Son (Luke, chapter 15).

Note the scenario of the parables. The Pharisees and scribes had come to Jesus and were murmuring about his association with sinners. Jesus taught these parables not only to justify his actions but to explain the great love his Father has for all of us.

The Lost Sheep   Jesus asked his antagonists the following question:

> "What man among you with a hundred sheep, losing one, would not leave the ninety-nine in the wilderness and go after the missing one till he found it? And when he found it, would he not joyfully take it on his shoulders?" (Lk 15:4-5).

Today, nomad tribes in Iran may well lose 20 to 40 percent of their flock while seeking new pastures. Their attitude toward the loss is one of quiet acceptance; they would not think of abandoning a whole flock to go after one lost sheep.

Imagine how nonsensical Jesus' question about the lost sheep must have seemed to his audience. A shepherd who would abandon his flock would be doing a foolish thing indeed. But that is the point of the parable—God the Father so loves us that he will go to every extreme to show his love for us. His love, especially for the lost, the sinner, goes beyond human comprehension. His love includes each and every person.

God's love is also tender. Note how the shepherd puts the

lost sheep on his shoulders. Why? Simply because lost sheep will lie down and refuse to move. The tender care and loving concern of this shepherd exemplifies the loving concern our Abba has for us.

The Lost Coin   Imagine your mother sweeping the whole house to find a small coin. Further imagine her announcing to the neighborhood that she found it and that everyone should rejoice. Perhaps you would conclude that your mother had "gone over the brink" as it were. The reactions of those who first heard Jesus' story might have been quite similar.

First, Jesus compared his Father to a woman—it was *unheard of* for a teacher to compare God to a woman. Second, he showed the great care with which the Father goes after the repentant sinner. The love of the Father far exceeds the normal expectations of the learned and holy men of Jesus' day. God's love is the cause of rejoicing.

The Lost Son   With the parable of the Good Samaritan, the parable of the Lost Son is perhaps the most familiar story in the New Testament. But the title which most of us know, "The Prodigal Son," obscures somewhat the main point of the parable. The focus of the parable is not the lost son. True, the younger son is prodigal in the sense of being profligate, exceedingly and recklessly wasteful with the patrimony he received from his father. He went as low as a person could go. Through his "eat, drink and be merry" kind of living, he ended up eating with pigs. For the Jew, Jesus could not have painted a more desolate picture.

But when the foolish son realized how low he had sunk, he repented, experienced a change of heart (metanoia) and returned to his father.

The father was waiting all the time. When the son comes into view, the father rushes out to him, embraces him and throws a wild celebration for him because he has returned. The father's love is prodigal, that is, foolishly spendthrift. It exceeds all expectation. The father is recklessly wasteful in his abundant love. He is the prodigal father.

The older brother complains. Like the Pharisee and the scribe, he is shocked that his father should be so foolish in his love for the sinner. The older brother, self-righteous to the end, is so perturbed that he does not even call his brother, "my brother," but rather refers to him as "this son of yours." But the father, still loving and wise in his ways, gently says to the angry son, "My son, you are with me always and all I have is yours. But it was only right we should celebrate and rejoice, because your brother here was dead and has come to life; he was lost and is found." Instead of reprimanding the older brother, the father delicately hears his complaint and lovingly asks him to reconsider. The focus of the parable is not on the wayward, nor on the faithful brother, but on the lavish love of the father who always stands ready to accept his children back into the family unconditionally and with great joy. So God loves us!

Jesus tells us that God's love goes beyond what we can ever possibly imagine. We do not earn it. It is a gift. It is always there. We need merely accept it as the 2-year-old stands ready to accept the love of his mommy and daddy. Indeed, Jesus invited his followers to call God Abba (daddy). He invites us to address God in the same intimate terms that he used.

This is the gospel! God loves us beyond what we can possibly imagine. He so loves us that he gives us more than the great gift of biological life, he gives us his Son. Jesus is trying to tell us through these parables of love and mercy that no matter what we do through life, no matter how we let ourselves down, no matter how many disappointments we bring to others and to our Father, our loving Abba awaits us with open arms like the father in the parable. He will rush out to greet us, put his arms around us and celebrate. All we need do is turn around, change our hearts and accept the bounteous love which is there. We should never forget this love and mercy brought to us by Jesus Christ. It is the heart of the good news!

LOVE AND FORGIVENESS

There are many conflicting ideas about love and forgiveness. Here are some of them. Check the place on the scale which represents your thinking on each of the following statements—1, strongly agree, to 5, strongly disagree.

1. "Love means never having to say you are sorry." —*Love Story*   1   2   3   4   5

2. We should forgive only when someone is genuinely sorry.   1   2   3   4   5

3. " 'I can forgive, but I cannot forget,' is only another way of saying, 'I can't forgive.' " —Henry Ward Beecher   1   2   3   4   5

4. The greatest sign of love is forgiveness—forgiveness with no strings attached.   1   2   3   4   5

5. "And forgive us our debts, as we have forgiven those who are in debt to us." —The *Our Father*   1   2   3   4   5

6. One of the hardest things to say is "I'm sorry."   1   2   3   4   5

7. "Love is love's reward." —John Dryden   1   2   3   4   5

8. "Never let your love for each other grow insincere, since *love covers over many a sin.*" —*First Letter of Peter*   1   2   3   4   5

Exercises:

1. Ask the most in-love couple you know to respond to these same statements. Why did they respond as they did?

2. Make a list of ways we express sorrow to each other (for example, an embrace, a gift, a kind word). What feelings do these symbols of love evoke in the one who receives them?

in the one who gives them? How do you react when someone expresses sorrow to you?

3. Write a short essay describing your best experience of either giving or receiving forgiveness.

4. As a class, plan a celebration of the sacrament of reconciliation to experience the Lord's forgiving touch.

5. Rewrite the parable of the Prodigal Son in a contemporary setting. Write it in the first person with you being the wayward son or daughter. Try to capture the joy of being accepted back.

   Alternative: With several classmates, dramatize your version of the Prodigal Son.

THE KINGDOM WILL TRIUMPH DESPITE ALL OPPOSITION TO IT

Jesus' message concerning the kingdom contains a great message of hope: Nothing can stop the kingdom's inevitable growth. The short parable of the Mustard Seed drives home this point. Jesus compares the kingdom of God to one of the smallest of seeds. From such small growth emerges a large shrub in which the birds of the air nest. From something extremely small, something quite large results. So it is with the growth of God's kingdom. And just as the birds find a home in the mustard tree, so too people from all over the world will find a place in God's kingdom.

The parable of the yeast or leaven also describes the pervasive effect of God's kingdom in the world. Jesus says:

> "It is like the yeast a woman took and mixed in with three measures of flour till it was leavened all through" (Lk 13:20-21).

A small amount of yeast causes a large amount of dough to rise. So, too, with God's kingdom. Something small and apparently insignificant has a quiet, though powerful and sure, effect on the world.

A third parable, the Parable of the Sower, stresses that nothing can prevent the spread of God's kingdom. The farmer in the story sowed seed on a footpath where some birds came along and ate it. He also scattered seed on rocky ground where it sprouted immediately but withered in the hot sun for lack of roots. He planted some among thorns where it was choked. But, finally, some of the seed did fall on good soil and produced a hundredfold.

Our first reaction to this parable might be that we are dealing with a stupid farmer. Who would sow seeds deliberately on paths, rocky ground and thorns? But this is only strange to us. In Israel, sowing came before the plowing of the field. The farmer intentionally sowed seed on his entire plot. He later plowed up the footpath and the withered thorns. He trusted that some of the seed would fall on the good soft earth he prepared. Further, it was impossible for him to avoid the rocks that jutted through the thin soil.

What is the point of the Parable of the Sower? In most of Jesus' parables, the point is found at the very end of the parable. In this case, the emphasis is on the harvest. Despite all the obstacles encountered by the seed, it will increase up to a hundredfold. This is really quite remarkable. A normal increase might be about thirtyfold. But a hundredfold? So it is with the kingdom of God. Despite every hindrance, failure and setback, God's reign of peace, justice, mercy and love will triumph! And it will triumph beyond anything we can possibly imagine.

REFLECTION

1. Think of some times in your life when good overcame the bad things that were happening to you. Did you need faith to get you through the tough times? Explain.

2. We live in an age when more and more people seem to be turning away from God. Do you agree that this is true? Explain. But, by the same token, Christians believe that there is evidence of God's kingdom all around us if we would but look. Think of some of the good things that are happening in our world—evidences of love, for example. Share these signs of God's kingdom with your classmates.

3. Mark explains the Parable of the Sower (Mk 4:3-20) as an allegory. An allegory takes every element in the story as a symbol which has a special meaning. If you haven't done so, read the parable.

   In Mark's allegory, the seed represents the word of God and the different kinds of ground correspond to different kinds of people who hear the word of God. Which kind of ground most accurately describes you?

   _____ footpath — accepts the word of God and then is easily tempted by Satan

   _____ rocky ground — joyous at first, then falters under pressure

   _____ thorns — desire for wealth and other cravings choke out faith

   _____ good soil — takes the gospel to heart and lets it yield a hundredfold

   • Which type of person would you like to be?
   • Which type of person do you think most Catholics are?

4. Read Mark 4:26-29, another parable about seed. Write your interpretation of this parable below. Share it with your classmates.

   _____

   _____

   _____

LIVE JOYFULLY

Belief in Jesus and his message should make us people of joy. We don't laugh our way through life ignoring the suffering and problems that are a very real part of our world, but we do have a profound sense of joy and peace. We believe that life has a purpose, that reality is fundamentally good, that God is love—generous, forgiving and saving. We believe that life will triumph over death. We believe God's kingdom is here now—although not yet fully established—and that it will come at the end of time in all of its glory.

Our attitude to the Lord's message should reflect the attitude of the man who found a buried treasure in the field:

> "The kingdom of heaven is like treasure hidden in a field which someone has found; he hides it again, goes off happy, sells everything he owns and buys the field" (Mt 13:44).

Or it might be like the merchant who searches for fine pearls.

> "When he finds one of great value he goes and sells everything he owns and buys it" (Mt 13:46).

Imagine the joy of the person who finds the valuable treasure or the priceless pearl or, today, wins a million dollars in a lottery. How much more should the Christian rejoice at hearing the good news of God's love for us! We should, like the person who found the treasure or the pearl, be willing to risk all for Jesus. We know that God is good, that we are loved beyond measure. What could be more valuable than this knowledge of the love of God?

Jesus teaches us that the time of decision is now. We should not wait around where he and his Father's kingdom are concerned. We should make the best of the good news we have heard, sharing the love we have been given and not keeping it to ourselves. We should not be like the man in the Parable of the Talents who refused to risk investing the money he had been given. We should act *now* because we never know when it will be too late, a lesson the foolish rich man described in Luke's gospel did not learn.

We have joy to share, to give to others; we let the love of the Lord touch us so we can touch others. Repent, believe the good news of God's salvation and live the love of the Lord—this is the message of Jesus Christ!

SUMMARY

1. Jesus taught that God's kingdom is here now. This kingdom refers to God's will for humanity being accomplished in the world—peace, justice and love extended to all, but especially to the poor, the oppressed and the downtrodden. Jesus wants us to reform our lives and to believe the good news about the coming of God's kingdom.

2. Jesus himself ushered in God's reign. His miracles, for example, powerfully demonstrate that salvation is here. The healing presence of the Lord Jesus Christ is a dramatic sign of the presence of God's kingdom.

3. The greatest sign of God's kingdom is his love for each of us. Jesus reveals that God is our loving Father, Abba, who forgives us and extends his merciful love to us.

4. There will be and are obstacles to God's work in the world. But Jesus teaches that despite these odds, the kingdom of God will inevitably triumph.

5. Because we have been privileged to hear the good news of God's love, we should risk everything for his kingdom. The time to decide is now. And because of this good news we should rejoice.

EXERCISES

1. Imagine that you have been commissioned to go preach the message of Jesus to nonbelievers in your neighborhood. Your task is to go from door to door and present the good news of Jesus.

   Construct a short outline of what you would say. What would you say first? What would you respond if someone said that you are preaching utter nonsense?

Share your outline with your classmates. Then discuss the following:

a. How would people probably react to you?

b. If they rejected you, would you be hurt? Explain.

c. Is the message of God's love too hard to believe? Why did so many people in our Lord's day reject it? Do people today really believe it?

d. Do you believe the gospel of Jesus? Explain.

2. *Some More Parables of Jesus.* Read the following parables. Briefly discuss what each means. Then match your interpretation of the parable with one of the five summary points presented on page 110.

Laborers in the Vineyard (Mt 20:1-16)   Summary point _____

The Good Samaritan (Lk 10:29-37)   Summary point _____

The Two Debtors (Lk 7:36-50)   Summary point _____

SCRIPTURE REFLECTION

He then told the guests a parable, because he had noticed how they picked the places of honor. He said this, "When someone invites you to a wedding feast, do not take your seat in the place of honor. A more distinguished person than you may have been invited, and the person who invited you both may come and say, 'Give up your place to this man.' And then, to your embarrassment, you would have to go and take the lowest place. No; when you are a guest, make your way to the lowest place and sit there, so that, when your host comes, he may say, 'My friend, move up higher.' In that way, everyone with you at the table will see you honored. For everyone who exalts himself will be humbled, and the man who humbles himself will be exalted" (Lk 14:7-11).

FIVE

Jesus in the Gospels

I am the bread of life.
He who comes to me will never be hungry;
he who believes in me will never thirst.
—John 6:35

We Christians hold that the New Testament is the living word of God which continually reveals the Lord Jesus and his message to us. It contains the gospel of Jesus—the good news of our redemption through the Son of God. This good news is the joyful announcement of all that Jesus said and accomplished as our Savior.

One way of approaching Jesus is to look carefully at him from each of the varying viewpoints of the authors of the gospels. The viewpoints of the evangelists (gospel writers) flowed from the particular needs of the audience for whom the author was writing. Only when we look at these different portraits of Jesus can we begin to appreciate better his richness and the way in which he touched people.

In this chapter, then, we will briefly discuss the following key images of Jesus that emerge from the four gospels:

1. Mark's Jesus: The Suffering Messiah
2. Matthew's Jesus: The New Moses
3. Luke's Jesus: The Universal Savior
4. John's Jesus: The Way to God

113

FOLLOWING JESUS

The four gospels challenge us to meet Jesus Christ and to follow him. Our Lord himself invites us when he says:

"If anyone wants to be a follower of mine,
let him renounce himself and take up his
cross and follow me" (Mk 8:34).

What does this verse mean to you? Respond by choosing the answer that is most meaningful at this time of your life.

1. To me, *taking up a cross* means:

____ a. doing boring things well

____ b. being mocked for doing the right thing

____ c. not giving in to peer pressure

____ d. _____

2. *Following Jesus* means:

____ a. nothing to me right now

____ b. I have heard something about him and am slightly interested in what he has to say

____ c. I am on the edge of the crowd looking at him and hoping to push my way closer to him

____ d. I'd be willing to die for him

____ e. _____

3. If I *renounced myself,* I would have to:

____ a. start thinking of others more, especially members of my family

____ b. stop being so lazy and start praying more

____ c. do things I don't like to do

____ d. _____

MARK'S JESUS: THE SUFFERING MESSIAH

Mark wrote the earliest gospel (perhaps around A.D. 65). His opening verse tells us about his fundamental belief:

> The beginning of the Good News about Jesus Christ, the Son of God (Mk 1:1).

Jesus is indeed the Son of God, and this is good news.

Scholars pretty much agree that the author of Mark was a disciple of St. Peter, and that the gospel contains some of what must have been Peter's early preaching. In Mark we find a certain vividness of detail that looks very much like an eyewitness account. His portrait of Jesus seems much more down-to-earth than in the other gospels.

Students of the gospels also believe that Mark wrote his gospel for a Christian community that was undergoing persecution. His aim was to comfort them with the gospel of Jesus and also to show that to follow Jesus means that Christians must suffer with him. Mark's gospel, then, presents a Suffering Messiah for Christians to imitate.

Mark's closeness to Peter and his desire to encourage his audience to imitate the Lord who suffered greatly affect the portrait of Jesus that emerges in his version of the good news. Let us point to a few examples.

A Down-to-earth Jesus   Mark believed that Jesus was the Son of God, but he believed in a *human* Jesus as well. For example, read Mark's version of the curing of the man with the withered hand:

> Then, grieved to find them so obstinate, he looked *angrily* round at them . . . (Mk 3:5, italics added).

Matthew and Luke soften this story by failing to mention that Jesus was angry.

Matthew and Luke, who had Mark in front of them as they composed their gospels, often tone down Mark's vivid details concerning Jesus, especially if those details tend to make Jesus look "too" human. Mark tells us that Jesus' relatives thought he was "out of his mind" (Mk 3:21); Matthew and Luke drop this detail. Mark tells us that Jesus "could work no miracle" in his home town except for a few cures because of the people's lack of faith (Mk 6:1-6). Luke drops this story—perhaps because he didn't want people to get the wrong idea about Jesus' power. Matthew changes the words "could not" to "did not"—"he did not work many miracles there because of their lack of faith" (Mt 13:58).

Mark's Jesus curses a fig tree (Mk 11:12-14) but also gently embraces the children who come to him (9:36). Here is the Son of God, but also a man of feeling and compassion.

The Suffering Messiah   Mark's gospel leaves us in no doubt that Jesus was the Messiah. Jesus accepts the claim when Peter proclaims, "You are the Christ" (Mk 8:30). But as we shall see in Chapter 7 when we study in more detail the titles of Jesus, our Lord's notion of what it meant to be the Christ (the Messiah) differed significantly from what most people of his day expected.

Jesus teaches that he came to suffer and to die for us. Three times he predicts his passion and death (Mk 8:31, 9:31, and 10:33-34). Jesus came to serve others. In a pivotal passage, Jesus says:

> "You know that among the pagans their so-called rulers lord it over them, and their great men make their authority felt. This is not to happen among you. No; anyone who wants to become great among you must be your servant, and anyone who wants to be first among you must be slave to all. For the Son of Man himself did not come to be served but to serve, and to give his life as a ransom for many" (Mk 10:42-45).

Mark's Jesus is truly the Son of God, but a Son whose life and death is our model. To follow Jesus means to pick up our daily cross in imitation of him. We should remember, though, that suffering for the Lord leads to our salvation and a participation in his glorious resurrection. This is why the good news is so good.

THE GOSPEL CHALLENGE

Read this passage from Mark and answer the questions which follow.

17 He was setting out on a journey when a man ran up, knelt before him and put this question to him, "Good master,
18 what must I do to inherit eternal life?" • Jesus said to him, "Why do you call me good?" No one is good but God
19 alone. • You know the commandments: *You must not kill; You must not commit adultery; You must not steal; You must not bring false witness; You must not defraud; Honor*
20 *your father and mother."* • And he said to him, "Master, I
21 have kept all these from my earliest days." • Jesus looked steadily at him and loved him, and he said, "There is one thing you lack. Go and sell everything you own and give the money to the poor, and you will have treasure in
22 heaven; then come, follow me." • But his face fell at these words and he went away sad, for he was a man of great wealth (Mk 10:17-22).

1. What problem might verse 18 pose?_____

_____

Read Matthew 19:16-18. How does Matthew solve this potential problem?

_____

How is this verse characteristic of Mark's portrait of Jesus?

_____

2. Jesus asks the young man if he knows the commandments. Do you? Give the corresponding number from our list of the commandments for the ones Jesus cited above:

_____

3. Why couldn't the young man follow Jesus?

_____

Do you think Jesus' love for the young man diminished any?

Explain. _____

4. Is there anything in your life that is keeping you from following Jesus Christ? If so, what?

_____

Discuss: Do you think the love of money keeps many people from following the Lord? Why or why not?

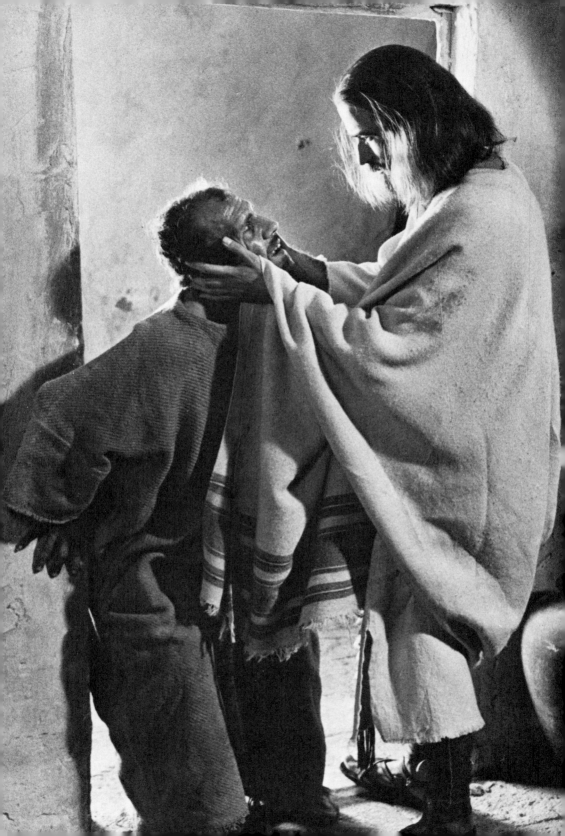

MATTHEW'S JESUS: THE NEW MOSES

Scholars date the writing of Matthew's gospel between A.D. 75 and A.D. 85. The author was a Jew, perhaps a scribe, who was very familiar with the customs and language of his people. The opening verse of the gospel clues us into the theological approach adopted by the author: "A genealogy of Jesus Christ, son of David, son of Abraham" (Mt 1:1). Matthew, whose audience was a community of Jews who had become Christians, wanted to demonstrate that the prophecies of the Hebrew scriptures are fulfilled in the person and work of Jesus—Jesus is indeed the promised son of David.

Matthew calls Jesus "Son of David" more than all the other gospels put together. This title would not be lost on a Jewish audience since it was a direct reference to the promised Messiah. In his effort to demonstrate that Jesus was truly the promised Messiah, Matthew also frequently cites Old Testament prophecies. Look at the following list to see how Matthew used the Old Testament:

Matthew		*Old Testament*
1:22-23	Jesus' birth of a virgin	Is 7:14
2:5-6	Born in Bethlehem	Mi 5:1
2:15	Flight into Egypt	Hos 11:1
2:18	Slaughter of the Innocents	Jer 31:15
4:15-16	Galilean ministry	Is 8:23—9:1
8:17	Miraculous cures	Is 53:4
12:18-21	Leadership of service	Is 42:1-4
13:14-15	Spiritual blindness	Is 6:9-10
13:35	Teaching in parables	Ps 78:2
21:5	Riding on a donkey	Is 62:11; Zec 9:9
27:9-10	Judas' betrayal	Zec 11:12-13

More than anything else, though, Matthew wishes to stress to his Jewish converts that Jesus is a new lawgiver, a *new Moses*. There are five main divisions in Matthew's gospel. Some scholars have said that Matthew arranged his gospel this way so that the reader could see that the gospel of Jesus Christ contains the New Law. The contrast is with the first five books of the Old Testament (the Pentateuch) which contains the Torah (Law) which the Jews received from Yahweh through Moses.

Of more significance is that Matthew deliberately collected together the ethical teachings of Jesus. These are found in the Sermon on the Mount, Matthew 5-7. Just as Moses of old handed down the Law from a mountain, so Jesus, the new Moses, hands down a new law from a mountain. These remarkable three chapters in Matthew's gospel present Jesus as an authoritative teacher who clearly knows that his Father's kingdom is here and wants to communicate what that means for his disciples.

Instead of giving another list of commandments, Jesus begins the Sermon on the Mount with eight beatitudes, statements of joy for people who try to do God's will. Here is a sampling of some of the most important sayings that appear in the Sermon on the Mount. They reveal God's will for us:

> "Love your enemies and pray for those who persecute you" (Mt 5:44).
>
> "You must therefore be perfect just as your heavenly Father is perfect" (Mt 5:48).
>
> "In your prayers do not babble as the pagans do. . . . Pray like this: Our Father in heaven . . ." (Mt 6:7,9).
>
> "You cannot be the slave both of God and of money" (Mt 6:24).
>
> "Do not judge, and you will not be judged" (Mt 7:1).
>
> "So always treat others as you would like them to treat you; that is the meaning of the Law and Prophets" (Mt 7:12).
>
> "It is not those who say to me, 'Lord, Lord,' who will enter the kingdom of heaven, but the person who does the will of my Father in heaven" (Mt 7:21).

Matthew's Jesus is a new Moses, a new lawgiver whose words contain the secret of salvation.

EXERCISES

1. Read the passages listed on page 119 which deal with the prophecies concerning Jesus. Note how each one points to the promised Messiah.

2. Discuss the meaning of each of the sayings from the Sermon on the Mount listed on page 120.

3. Read the Sermon on the Mount, Matthew 5-7. Select five sayings other than those given above which you especially like. Share one (or more) with your classmates and explain why you like it.

4. *Beatitudes.* Jesus calls us to be "beatitude people." Read the beatitudes section again (Mt 5:3-12). Mark how well each of the following traits describes you.

> 4 — this describes me very well
> 3 — this describes me most of the time
> 2 — this describes me some of the time
> 1 — I need to work on this

_____ poor in spirit

_____ gentle

_____ hungry and thirsty for justice

_____ merciful

_____ pure in heart

_____ peacemaker

_____ willing to suffer for the right

Discuss:

1. As a class, work up a definition for each of these traits.

2. Share at least one occasion when *you* exhibited one of the traits to a high degree.

3. Mention some factors in our society that work against each of these traits.

LUKE'S JESUS: THE UNIVERSAL SAVIOR

Luke, a companion of the great Christian missionary St. Paul, probably wrote his gospel sometime between A.D. 75 and A.D. 85. He dedicated his gospel to a certain Theophilus with the purpose of assuring him "how well founded the teaching is that you have received" (Lk 1:4).

The teaching that Luke specifically zeroes in on is that Jesus has brought salvation to *all* people. Writing for a Gentile-Christian audience, Luke emphasized that Jesus is a compassionate Savior who came to save Gentile as well as Jew, poor as well as rich, sick and healthy alike. Luke's Jesus is the universal Messiah who brings the healing love of God to everyone.

Luke's Jesus showed special affection for the people who lived on the edge of society, the people we would call "losers"; for example, he cured lepers, people who could not even approach others without ringing a bell to warn of their disease. He even singled out as an example the one leper who returned to thank him—a Samaritan. And it is only Luke's gospel that records the famous parable of the Good Samaritan, the model of love toward neighbor.

Jesus associated with tax collectors, often dining with them. He even accepted dinner invitations from the Pharisees. He did not reject the wealthy, but extended his love to them.

Luke's Jesus displayed revolutionary attitudes toward women. Women in our Lord's day were second-class citizens. Jesus' attitude toward them showed that God, through his Son, showered his love on them. Women felt free to approach Jesus. The woman with a flow of blood touched him; another woman rushed in off the street to anoint his feet and ask for his forgiveness; still others comforted him in his own time of afflic-tion. Women were Jesus' constant companions and his disciples. Martha and Mary were his friends. His mother Mary plays a unique role in Luke's gospel, serving as the model of faith in God and what he accomplishes through his Son.

Jesus is a compassionate Savior who, in his dying moments, promised a reward to the good thief and forgave his enemies. His love includes everyone and excludes no one. An essential ingredient of Luke's message about Jesus is that we should imitate our Lord. It is in his gospel that we find the parables of the lost sheep, the lost coin and the lost son. The Father's compassion for the "losers" in society shines forth through his Son, Jesus Christ. We should let Jesus' love shine forth through us as well.

COMPASSION

Read Luke 19:1-10. Then answer the following questions:

1. Why did people complain about Jesus associating with Zacchaeus?
2. Why did Jesus assure Zacchaeus of salvation?
3. How does this passage support the view that Jesus was compassionate?

Discuss

1. As a class, define the term *compassion*.
2. Make a list of the kinds of people in today's world who are most in need of our Lord's compassion.
3. Can you and your classmates help any of the people on your list? How?

JOHN'S JESUS: THE WAY TO GOD

Written sometime in the last decade of the first century, John's gospel presents a highly developed reflection on the meaning and person of Jesus. Whereas Mark, Matthew and Luke wrote their gospels for relatively new converts, John's audience was quite familiar with the basics of the good news. Thus John seems more concerned with reflecting on the theological significance of Jesus.

John's basic stance toward Jesus is apparent from the opening verses of his gospel:

In the beginning was the Word:
the Word was with God
and the Word was God.
The Word was the true light

that enlightens all men;
and he was coming into the world.

The Word was made flesh,
he lived among us,
and we saw his glory,
the glory that is his as the only Son of the Father,
full of grace and truth (Jn 1:1,9,14).

Reflected in this opening prologue is John's typical way of approaching Jesus. His reflection on Jesus is known as a "descending Christology." The descending Christology in John's gospel has the following pattern:

1. Jesus is identified as God. In this case he is called "the Word" and the Word is identified as God. He is also called "the only Son of the Father." From the beginning, it is quite clear that Jesus is a divine person.

2. The Son of God becomes man. He lives with us.

3. The Son of God reveals who God is; he enlightens us, "the Word was true light."

4. By looking at Jesus, the Word of God and the only Son of God, we can learn about the Father.

The value of this approach to Jesus is that he can clearly be presented as the Way to the Father. Consider the following quotations:

"Whatever the Father does the Son does too"
(Jn 5:19).

"If you did know me, you would know my Father as well" (Jn 8:19).

"When you have lifted up the Son of Man,
then you will know that I am He" (Jn 8:28).

"The Father and I are one" (Jn 10:30).

"Whoever sees me,
sees the one who sent me" (Jn 12:45).

"To have seen me is to have seen the Father"
(Jn 14:9).

John's Jesus is trustworthy. He is clearly God. Thus he becomes for us the way, the truth and the life. Jesus is the bread of life, living water, the sheepgate, the good shepherd, the resurrection and the life, the true vine, the light of the world. As his disciples we should listen to and believe what he has to say. We should imitate him and join ourselves to him. In that way, we are promised eternal life:

> "I am the resurrection.
> If anyone believes in me, even though he dies he
>   will live,
> and whoever lives and believes in me
> will never die" (Jn 11:25-26).

BREAD OF LIFE

Please read John 6 where Jesus calls himself the "bread of life." Jesus wants us to know that he will meet all of our human needs and that he will fulfill our lives.

Personal Inventory. How much do you look to the Lord as the source of your life? Rank yourself from 1 to 3 on the following areas of spiritual growth.

    1 — This describes me pretty well
    2 — I need some improvement here
    3 — I have a lot of work to do on this item

Things: I enjoy the good things that come my way—for example, my personal possessions—but I know that they will never be the source of my happiness.

    1   2   3

Scripture: I derive nourishment from reading the word of God in the Bible.

    1   2   3

Eucharist: I receive the Eucharist frequently and participate in the Mass weekly.

    1   2   3

Prayer: I ask the Lord for help when I need it.

    1   2   3

Gratitude: I occasionally thank the Lord for the life he has given me, for my family, friends, health, education and the like.

    1   2   3

Bread for others: Just as the Lord is bread for me, I try to be a source of life for others. For example, I try to listen to their needs and respond to them.

    1   2   3

SUMMARY

1. There is only one gospel, that is, the good news of God accomplished in the person of Jesus Christ. But we typically speak of four versions of the good news as the four gospels.

2. Each of the evangelists emphasizes something different about Jesus. This is partly due to the audiences for whom they were writing. The various portraits of Jesus contained in the four gospels give us a richer image of Jesus.

3. Mark presents a human Jesus. In writing to a suffering Christian community, Mark stressed the fact that Jesus was a Suffering Messiah and that his disciples must also be prepared to suffer.

4. Matthew portrays Jesus as a Messiah who fulfilled all the Old Testament prophecies made about him. In particular, he portrays Jesus as a new lawgiver—a New Moses—who hands down the law of love in the Sermon on the Mount.

5. Luke gives us a universal Messiah, one who is compassionate to all people, but especially to those people whom we might consider "losers."

6. John's Jesus is preeminently the way to the Father. As God's Son and Word, he reveals to us what God is like. To see Jesus is to see the Father.

EXERCISE

Select any five chapters from one of the four gospels, preferably chapters you haven't read yet. Read these chapters. On the basis of your reading, write a short essay in which you explain how the particular evangelist portrays Jesus in these chapters. Try to boil it down to one outstanding image of Jesus.

SCRIPTURE REFLECTION

Blessed be God the Father of our Lord Jesus Christ,
who has blessed us with all the spiritual blessings of
    heaven in Christ.
Before the world was made, he chose us, chose us in
    Christ,
to be holy and spotless, and to live through love in his
    presence,
determining that we should become his adopted sons,
    through Jesus Christ
for his own kind purposes,
to make us praise the glory of his grace,
his free gift to us in the Beloved,
in whom, through his blood, we gain our freedom, the
    forgiveness of our sins.
Such is the richness of the grace
which he has showered on us
in all wisdom and insight (Eph 1:3-8).

SIX

The Passion, Death and Resurrection of Jesus

In the evening of that same day, the first day of the week, the doors were closed in the room where the disciples were, for fear of the Jews. Jesus came and stood among them. He said to them, "Peace be with you," and showed them his hands and his side. The disciples were filled with joy when they saw the Lord, and he said to them again, "Peace be with you.

"As the Father sent me,
so am I sending you."

—John 20:19-21

One of the most important symbols for Christians is the cross. When you think about it, it is rather ironic that this symbol—the sign of a criminal, of defeat and death—has become loaded with so much meaning. In his letter to the Galatians St. Paul speaks about the "scandal of the cross" (Gal 5:11). To nonbelievers the cross was a foolish sign of a foolish people who put their faith in a condemned criminal.

But for Christians the cross is a powerful symbol of the mystery of God's incredible love for us. Through our Lord's sacrifice we have become reconciled to the Father. Jesus' passion, death, resurrection and glorification are for us the great paschal mystery of God's love. The death on a cross leads to a resurrection of superabundant life. Our Lord shares this life with us. A symbol of total defeat has become for us a symbol of victory over sin and death.

This chapter will look at the events of Holy Week —specifically the passion, death and resurrection of Jesus—and discuss their significance for Christian life. These events are at the heart of our faith in Jesus Christ.

129

SCRIPTURE READING

To prepare for this chapter, prayerfully read the four accounts of Jesus' passion and death. Make a list of five things that impressed you during your reading. Share these with your classmates.

Mark 14-15   Luke 22-23

Matthew 26-27   John 18-19

THE PASSION NARRATIVE

The Preliminaries

The events of Holy Week began on a high note. Jesus entered Jerusalem in triumph, allowing the people to proclaim him as the promised Messiah. They hailed him with palm branches and spread their cloaks before him as they shouted:

> "Blessings on the King who comes,
> in the name of the Lord!
> Peace in heaven
> and glory in the highest heavens!" (Lk 19:38).

Jesus spent the early days of the week teaching in the Temple. His teaching once again raised the ire of some of the leaders. Matthew reports:

> Then the chief priests and the elders of the people assembled . . . and made plans to arrest Jesus by some trick and have him put to death. They said, however, "It must not be during the festivities; there must be no disturbance among the people" (Mt 26:3-5).

The festivities revolved around the feast of the Passover, the great Jewish celebration of liberation from Egypt in the days of Moses. Jesus gathered his disciples and celebrated with them a new Passover, a freeing from both sin and death accomplished by his own death and resurrection. In this special meal Jesus gave himself to his friends in the form of bread and wine; he instituted the Eucharist as a sign of love—his unselfish sacrifice on the cross for us. The Eucharist represents Jesus' free and total gift of life poured out for us. At this meal he instructed his disciples and all of his future followers:

> "I give you a new commandment:
> love one another;
> just as I have loved you,
> you also must love one another.
> By this love you have for one another,
> everyone will know that you are my disciples"
> (Jn 13:34-35).

The Garden and the Arrest

All the gospels report that Judas, one of the Twelve, sneaked off to the chief priests and plotted with them to hand Jesus over.

> He . . . looked for an opportunity to betray him to
> them without the people knowing (Lk 22:6).

Judas' opportunity came when Jesus retired to the Garden of Gethsemane to seek the strength to endure his coming suffering and death. Jesus prayed that he might be delivered from death. Like any normal human he recoiled from death, especially one that would be excruciatingly painful. But he prayed that his Father's will be done. Jesus accepted death because he knew it was the greatest sign of love.

> "A man can have no greater love
> than to lay down his life for his friends" (Jn 15:13).

At any rate, Jesus' foes grasped their opportunity by arresting him away from the crowds and under cover of darkness. At the moment of Jesus' arrest his disciples sought to defend him. But to the end he rejected power plays; he even healed the ear of a servant who was injured in the scuffle and told Peter:

> "Put your sword back, for all who draw the sword
> will die by the sword" (Mt 26:52).

The Trial Before the Jewish Leaders

If we compare and contrast the gospel accounts of the trial

before the Sanhedrin, there is some confusion about whether there was a preliminary hearing *and* a trial, and whether one or the other took place late Thursday night or in the wee hours of Good Friday morning. The evangelists, writing a generation or so after the events, were interested in reporting the charges against Jesus, not in presenting the finer points of the Jewish and Roman judicial process.

And what were those charges? Even before Holy Week the leaders of the Jews considered Jesus a threat to the civil order as well as a danger to their own religious supremacy.

> "If we let him go on in this way everybody will believe in him, and the Romans will come and destroy the Holy Place and our nation" (Jn 11:48).

The high priest Caiaphas had clearly stated that Jesus had to be eliminated:

> "It is better for one man to die for the people, than for the whole nation to be destroyed" (Jn 11:50).

All that remained, then, was for Jesus to be convicted of a crime that required death under Jewish law: blasphemy.

Now, at his trial, false witnesses appeared against Jesus, but these witnesses could not even agree on what Jesus had actually said, let alone what he meant. They were of no use in convicting Jesus.

The leaders also focused on Jesus' words:

> "Destroy this sanctuary, and in three days I will raise it up" (Jn 2:19).

Jesus, of course, was talking not about the Jerusalem Temple, but about his own body. These words were also insufficient as evidence against him.

Finally, because no conclusive evidence could be produced, the high priest Caiaphas asked Jesus a direct question:

> "Are you the Christ . . . the Son of the Blessed One?"

Jesus firmly responded:

> "I am . . . And you will see *the Son of Man seated at
> the right hand of the Power* and *coming with the
> clouds of heaven*" (Mk 14:61-62).

Jesus was clearly claiming to be the Messiah-king and the
prophet Daniel's mysterious Son of Man who was to usher in
God's kingdom. His own words provided the Sanhedrin with the
evidence it needed to convict him of blasphemy. Caiaphas tore
his robe and said:

> "You heard the blasphemy. What is your finding?"
> And they all gave their verdict: he deserved to die
> (Mk 14:63).

The Roman Trial

Under Jewish law, the Sanhedrin had the power to declare
the death sentence for crimes, including the crime of blasphemy.
(*An American Catholic Catechism* defines blasphemy as "intentionally insulting or denying the goodness of God." The
Sanhedrin believed that Jesus insulted God by his claims.) As we
noted in Chapter 2, however, under the Roman law of occupation
only the Roman court could carry out the death penalty. Thus the
Sanhedrin was forced to turn Jesus over to the Roman governor,
Pontius Pilate, for trial. The leaders said to Pilate: "We have a Law
. . . and according to that Law he ought to die, because he
claimed to be the Son of God" (Jn 19:7).

Since Roman occupying forces were disinterested in the internal religious disputes of their subjects, however, the Sanhedrin
had to portray Jesus as a criminal under Roman law. Hence the
leaders made the following charge:

> "We found this man inciting our people to revolt,
> opposing payment of the tribute to Caesar, and
> claiming to be Christ, a king" (Lk 23:2).

The gospels report that Pilate saw through this ploy. He
knew that Jesus was innocent and appears to have wanted to free
him. He even sent him to Herod Antipas who—like Pilate—was in
Jerusalem for the Passover feast. But Herod, who found Jesus a
bothersome novelty rather than a threat to the empire, merely
mocked Jesus and sent him back to Pilate.

Pilate now tried to manipulate the crowd to attain his own ends: to free Jesus and, perhaps more important to Pilate, to avoid freeing Barabbas, a known revolutionary. He offered the crowd a choice: He would free either Jesus or Barabbas. The crowd picked Barabbas and demanded that Jesus be executed. The situation was getting out of hand. Pilate ordered Jesus scourged, itself a terrible and often fatal punishment, thinking the crowd might then be satisfied. It was not, and Pilate finally gave in to the demands for the death sentence.

The synoptic gospels report that Pilate went against his conscience; he knew that Jesus was innocent, but he gave in to mob pressure. Pilate seems motivated primarily by self-interest and expediency. In John's gospel Pilate is anxious to release Jesus until Jesus' enemies shout:

> "If you set him free you are no friend of Caesar's; anyone who makes himself king is defying Caesar" (Jn 19:12).

This threat hit home; no official would be safe who showed sympathy to someone who might challenge the emperor.

In a famous scene Pilate washed his hands of the whole bothersome mess. He turned Jesus over to be crucified, but, to mock the Jews, he posted this notice on Jesus' cross:

JESUS THE NAZARENE, KING OF THE JEWS

The supreme irony is that Jesus *is* the king of the Jews and of all humanity!

COURAGE

The Passion narratives tell the story of a courageous man, one who could have easily backed away from the charges against him.

These narratives prompt Jesus' followers to imitate him—to be courageous under the most trying of times.

How courageous are you? How do you suffer for the Lord? Here are some situations in which you may have found yourself or situations which you may encounter in the future. Respond as honestly as you can.

_____ 1. Almost everyone is cheating on a test. I would: a. not cheat; b. cheat; c. I don't know.

_____ 2. My friends are encouraging me to go along with something I know is wrong. I would: a. decline; b. probably go along with the crowd; c. I'm not sure.

_____ 3. At a party someone is making fun of Catholics. I would: a. publicly defend my religion; b. remain silent; c. I don't know.

Can you add a couple of situations to this list which, from your experience, would take some courage on your part?

_____ 4. _____

_____

_____

_____ 5. _____

_____

_____

Discuss:

1. Why would each of the examples above demand courage? Would they also involve some degree of suffering?

2. Who is the most courageous person you and your classmates know? What makes this person this way?

Read: Matthew 27:3-10 and Acts 1:15-22. Discuss the following:

1. What do you notice about these two accounts?

2. If you had the chance to speak to Judas as he was contemplating suicide, what would you say to him?

The Crucifixion of Jesus

Someone once said that the way a person dies punctuates the sentence of his or her life. It summarizes all that the person has said and accomplished. If there is any truth to this statement, then Jesus' life ended as he lived: in total, loving service of others. His final mark is an exclamation point of love.

Jesus' journey to Calvary shows him concerned not for himself, but for others. He tells the women who mourn for him,

> "Daughters of Jerusalem, do not weep for me;
> weep rather for yourselves and for your children"
> (Lk 23:28).

Jesus' prayer for them was that they be spared the suffering that would come to those who would be alive in the last days.

Jesus' fate was to be crucified on a small hill outside the city gates of Jerusalem. Crucifixion was an excruciating and humiliating method of capital punishment. *The New Catholic Encyclopedia* gives us a feeling for what Jesus underwent:

> The Romans considered crucifixion so shameful a penalty that it could not be inflicted on Roman citizens. Roman crucifixion was always preceded by a scourging of the victim at the place of judgment. Then the criminal, still naked after the scourging, was made to carry his own cross (that is, the crossbeam) to the place of execution, where he was exposed to public ridicule and death. . . . The full weight of the body hanging by the arms would prevent the right functioning of the lungs and so cause death by asphyxiation after not too long a time. Therefore, to prolong the agony of the victim, support was given to his body by a kind of seat block and by binding or nailing his feet to the cross. Death could be hastened by breaking the victim's legs, so that shock and asphyxiation soon ended his life. Sometimes, however, the side and heart would be pierced by a spear to cause immediate death.

Jesus must have suffered much during his scourging. We know he was unable to complete carrying his crossbeam, and

Simon of Cyrene was pressed into service to assist him. According to the Jewish custom, at the site of the crucifixion Jesus was offered a drugged wine to help dull the pain. He refused, wanting to be clear-headed to the end and to feel the full effects of the suffering he chose to undergo for us.

Jesus' last words, as recorded by the evangelists, typify the way he lived. They are reported below with a brief note on their theological significance.

"Father, forgive them; they do not know what they are doing" (Lk 23:34)

In his dying moments, Jesus exhibited the loving forgiveness that characterized his entire ministry. He died as he lived.

"Indeed, I promise you, today you will be with me in paradise" (Lk 23:43)

The good thief is assured of salvation on the very day it was accomplished for all of us. Jesus thought of others in his own terrible moment of agony.

"Woman, this is your son. . . . This is your mother" (Jn 19:26,27)

Jesus showed concern for his mother in his dying moments. He entrusted his mother to the church, represented by the apostle John. Thus, by Jesus' desire, Mary is Mother of the Church.

"My God, my God, why have you deserted me?" (Mt 27:46)

Here Jesus was praying Psalm 22, not despairing as some of the bystanders thought. We should understand that he probably prayed the entire psalm which ultimately proclaims God's mercy to his Suffering Servant.

"I am thirsty" (Jn 19:28)

John includes these words to show that Jesus fulfilled the prophecy about the Messiah in Psalm 69, "When I was thirsty they gave me vinegar to drink." Jesus accepted death and willingly tasted the last bitter drop of its agony until his Father's will was fulfilled.

"It is accomplished" (Jn 19:30)

What was accomplished was the plan of salvation for all people. Jesus allowed sin and death to overcome him. But by his resurrection, he overpowered them. God's will for Jesus included his death but it also included the magnificent resurrection to superabundant life and the remission of sin through his Son.

"Father, into your hands I commit my spirit" (Lk 23:46)

Jesus quotes Psalm 31. Jesus entrusted his life to his Father in an act of supreme faith and love. Jesus stands for us all; he feared death but trusted in his Father to rescue him out of the depths. He gave to his Father, on our behalf, his very life. Thus his death becomes for us the perfect symbol of God's love.

Jesus hung on the cross for several hours. It was approaching evening and a new day according to the Jewish way of reckoning time. Since both the Sabbath and the Passover were about to begin, the Jews petitioned the Romans for permission to hasten the death of the condemned men and to bury them. When the soldiers got to Jesus, he was already dead. To make sure, one of the soldiers pierced Jesus' side. Blood and water flowed out.

Joseph of Arimathea, a follower of Jesus and a member of the Sanhedrin, received permission to bury Jesus. He was wrapped in a white linen cloth and buried in a tomb hewn out of rock.

The passion of Jesus was over. And as the synoptic gospels note, a new age had begun. The Temple curtain ripping in two symbolized that the old covenant was finished and a new covenant sealed in the blood of Jesus Christ was now in effect. This new covenant leads to the remission of sin and the resurrection of the dead.

Meanwhile, the disciples huddled in fear in a room, and the women prepared to anoint Jesus' hastily buried body.

STATIONS OF THE CROSS

The Stations of the Cross is a traditional Catholic devotion. The stations are meditations on the major events of the passions and death of Jesus, usually in the presence of religious art that depicts the events.

Create a modern-day version of the stations:

1. Select several of the following New Testament scenes.
2. Find pictures from magazines or create your own artwork to illustrate them.
3. Compose a short prayer for each station. Make it something meaningful for you.

Possible scenes

Gethsemane	The scourging
Judas' betrayal	Carrying the cross
Jesus' arrest	The crucifixion
Jesus' trial	

Add to this list if you care to. Be sure to share your stations with your classmates, perhaps even taking turns reciting them.

THE RESURRECTION OF JESUS

The resurrection of Jesus is absolutely essential to our salvation and to our faith in Jesus. Without our Lord's resurrection, there would be no church. As St. Paul wrote to the Corinthians:

> "If Christ has not been raised then our preaching is useless and your believing it is useless" (1 Cor 15:14).

Something dramatic and unparalleled in human history happened on the Sunday morning after Passover. The gospels do not describe the resurrection itself—no one, in fact, witnessed it—but they and the rest of the New Testament do record the impact it made on the frightened disciples who were hiding in an upper room. Their lives literally changed. With the gift of the Holy Spirit given to them on Easter/Pentecost, they went out to share with the Jews and the rest of the world the good news: Jesus of Nazareth lives! We have seen him! He has conquered death! He is the Messiah, the Lord, the Son of God! Repent and believe!

St. Peter's proclamation on Pentecost Sunday summarizes the incredible good news about Jesus Christ:

> "Men of Israel, listen to what I am going to say: Jesus the Nazarene was a man commended to you by God by the miracles and portents and signs that God worked through him when he was among you, as you all know. This man, who was put into your power by the deliberate intention and foreknowledge of God, you took and had crucified by men outside the Law. You killed him, but God raised him to life, freeing him from the pangs of Hades; for it was impossible for him to be held in its power. . . .
>
> "God raised this man Jesus to life, and all of us are witnesses to that.
>
> "For this reason the whole House of Israel can be certain that God has made this Jesus whom you crucified both Lord and Christ" (Acts 2:22-24, 32,36).

ORIGINAL RESEARCH

To appreciate our theological reflection on the resurrection, it is most important for you to see firsthand what the New Testament says about the resurrection. Thus, please do the following exercise very carefully.

1. Divide the class into four groups. Each group should select for *careful* reading and studying one of the following resurrection texts:

   a. Mark 16:1-20   c. Luke 24:1-53
   b. Matthew 28:1-20   d. John 20:1-31

2. Then, on separate paper, make a chart listing the events and people in the text you read:

List events (with some key details)	List the people who see Jesus

3. Read 1 Corinthians 15:3-8. Note the people to whom Jesus appears in this early creed Paul is quoting.

4. On the board or on a large chart, compare and contrast your lists. Note similarities and differences.

5. Discuss these questions:

   a. Do the differences in the resurrection stories argue for or against their truth? Explain your answers.

b. In our Lord's day the Jewish law did not legally acknowledge women witnesses. Is it significant that women
   discovered the empty tomb, and that in John's gospel
   Jesus appears first to Mary Magdalene? How might this
   support the truth of the resurrection?

c. How do we *know* that Jesus rose from the dead?

d. If the Emmaus story is literally true, what might Jesus
   have told the disciples?

e. Was it reasonable for Thomas to doubt that Jesus rose?
   Explain.

Questioning What Happened

The claim of Peter and the early Christians that Jesus actually rose from the dead has confounded people from the very start
of Christianity. Even in the time of the apostles some of the
Jewish leaders circulated the story that Jesus' disciples stole his
body and fabricated the story of his resurrection.

Believing Christians, of course, thoroughly reject this theory
of apostolic fraud. It is the argument of nonbelievers. The way we
respond to this theory is to ask these questions: What would the
apostles gain from making up the resurrection stories? Why
would they be willing to die for a lie? Many early Christians suffered unbelievable torture and death for their absolute conviction
that Jesus rose from the dead, that he was the Son of God. If this
were a lie why would so many give up their lives to affirm it? The
martyrdom of so many early Christians argues very, very strongly
for the truth of Jesus' resurrection.

Other theories which deny the reality of the resurrection are
common today. For example, some people who are familiar with
pre-Christian religious beliefs claim that the resurrection event is
merely a story, that it is similar to the spring fertility rites and
myths associated with pagan gods like Attis, Adonis, Osiris and
Dionysus. Thus Christianity is only one of several early religions;
there is nothing especially unique about it.

Others interpret the resurrection as a *symbol* that the spirit
of Jesus lives on, or that his message and influence survived his

death. They do not think the resurrection was a physical reality or that the resurrection stories were meant to be taken literally.

How does the believer respond to these theories? Is there anything to say to those who hold that the resurrection is just a story from an early religion or that it is merely symbolic of Jesus' continuing influence in the world?

The resurrection varies markedly from the myths associated with the pagan religions. First of all, the resurrection concerns a historical person, Jesus of Nazareth. Secondly, it had nothing to do with spring fertility rites; its meaning had nothing in common with the change of seasons element of the pagan religions.

Interpreting the resurrection as a symbol totally ignores the insistence of St. Paul and the evangelists that Jesus was *seen* by the disciples.

> He appeared first to Cephas and secondly to the Twelve. Next he appeared to more than five hundred of the brothers at the same time, most of whom are still alive, though some have died; then he appeared to James, and then to all the apostles; and last of all he appeared to me too (1 Cor 15:5-8).

Thomas didn't believe until he was invited to touch the Lord. Jesus even cooked and ate some fish to show that he was real.

The gospel accounts talk of an empty tomb. But the empty tomb led only to wonderment; it did not lead to faith in the resurrected Jesus. Only the appearances of Jesus to his friends led them to the absolute conviction that the Father glorified his Son. Jesus' body was dramatically transformed to a superabundant life. Jesus lives on.

Through the experiences they had of Jesus after his death, the apostles were convinced that he was both Son of Man and Son of God, the Lord and Messiah. He was not a corpse which came back to life (like Lazarus), nor was he a hallucination or ghost. As scripture scholar Father Raymond Brown writes:

> . . . Christians can and indeed should continue to speak of a *bodily* resurrection of Jesus. Our earliest ancestors in the faith proclaimed a

bodily resurrection in the sense that they did not think that Jesus' body corrupted in the tomb. However, and this is equally important, Jesus' risen body was no longer a body as we know bodies, bound by the dimensions of space and time. It is best to follow Paul's description of risen bodies as spiritual, not natural or physical.[1]

RESURRECTION AND YOU

Christian belief in Jesus' resurrection is at the heart of our religion. We believe two things: 1) God has bestowed on Jesus the fullness of life which is his due as both Son of God and Son of Man; 2) Jesus' resurrection demonstrates what God will do for us. The Father who raised Jesus will raise us.

How strongly do you believe in our Lord's resurrection and what does it mean to you? Try the following exercises.

Read John 20:19-29. Answer the following:

1. Explain how you are either like or unlike Thomas.

   _____

   _____

2. Is it ever a good thing to be a doubter? Explain.

   _____

   _____

3. Check your response to this statement: "Happy are those who have not seen and yet believe" (Jn 20:29).

   _____ describes me well

   _____ I'm not sure about this

   _____ doesn't describe me

4. *Discuss:*

   a. Agree to definitions of both *doubt* and *faith.*

   b. Is it possible to convince others that Jesus rose from the dead? Why or why not?

---

1. Raymond E. Brown, *The Virginal Conception & Bodily Resurrection of Jesus* (New York: Paulist Press, 1973), pp. 127-128.

THE MEANING OF THE PASCHAL MYSTERY

What is the significance of the suffering, death and resurrection of Jesus Christ? What does it mean for us?

We begin with the mystery of the incarnation, that is, God becoming man in the person of his Son, Jesus Christ. We believe that the Word became flesh and lived with us because of the Father's great love for us. He became one with us to communicate with us. And what he has communicated is life itself.

As the Word of God who came to show us the way to the Father, Jesus taught us love and forgiveness. He wishes us to imitate God himself. St. John wrote:

My dear people
let us love one another since love comes from
     God
and everyone who loves is begotten by God and
     knows God" (1 Jn 4:7).

The Son's assumption of a human nature in itself is a supreme act of love. The perfect God entered into a human condition riddled with sin and alienated from the source of life.

Christ Jesus freely allowed this sinful condition to destroy him. Why? He did it out of obedience to his Father and out of the deepest love for us, his friends. He taught that the greatest sign of love is to die for one's friends. Jesus endured the greatest evil that can befall us as individuals—death—to demonstrate the extent of his love for us. And this great love brought salvation to us. Death died when Jesus died and rose from the dead.

Through the Lord's sacrifice on the cross, he "passed over" from this sinful world to his Father. He was the Paschal Lamb (*paschal* means "passover") offered to the Father to atone for sins. The resurrection completes the passover to the Father. Thus, both Jesus' death *and* resurrection accomplish our salvation. Together they comprise the great paschal mystery of God's love for us through our Lord Jesus Christ.

Christian faith is a paschal faith, a faith in the fact of the resurrection through which sin and death have been conquered and our eternal salvation won. The Christian believes that Jesus is the resurrection and the life. Those who have faith in him will be raised on the last day. St. Paul underscores the importance of this great mystery of God's love when he writes:

> For if the dead are not raised, Christ has not been raised, and if Christ has not been raised, you are still in your sins. And what is more serious, all who have died in Christ have perished. If our hope in Christ has been for this life only, we are the most unfortunate of all people (1 Cor 15:16-19).

Living the Paschal Mystery

We Christians have the rare privilege and serious responsibility to live both the cross of Jesus and his resurrection in our daily lives. We must allow the Lord to touch us and live through us. We live the paschal mystery of God's love through our baptism and the Eucharist. We live the paschal mystery when we respond to Christ's command to go into the world, preach the good news, love and forgive others.

We meet Christ in baptism when we die to sin and rise to a new life with him.

> We must realize that our former selves have been crucified with him to destroy this sinful body and to free us from the slavery of sin (Rom 6:6).

Baptism is not something we receive once and for all; it is a daily call to renew ourselves and be reborn in the Holy Spirit. It is a call to pick up the crosses that come into our lives—the pain and suffering involved in doing the right thing and being faithful to the Lord.

We celebrate God's love each week in the liturgy of the Mass. The Eucharist is a celebration and remembrance of the Lord's death and resurrection. The Eucharist is an invitation to receive the living Lord and share him with each of our fellow Christians and all people. The Eucharist is a reminder that we must break ourselves as Jesus did but also celebrate joyfully the great life that has been given to us because of his sacrifice.

The Lord calls us to share the good news of God's love with

others. Before he ascended into heaven, that is, returned in full glory to his Father, Jesus commanded his followers to go out into the world to make disciples; to baptize in the name of the Father, the Son and the Holy Spirit; to teach everyone to observe all the commands that he taught. And the Lord Jesus promised to be with us, his disciples, forever. We live the death and resurrection of Jesus when we attempt to obey these commands.

John's gospel gives a tremendous insight into how we should live the paschal mystery. When Jesus appeared to the apostles on Easter Sunday he gave them the gift of the Holy Spirit. With the Spirit the power of God's love is unleashed among us. Jesus commanded his disciples:

"As the Father sent me,
so am I sending you" (Jn 20:21).

One who is sent is a missionary. As followers of Jesus we are missionaries who are sent into the world with the Spirit as our guide to share God's love with others.

A key missionary task is to share with others the forgiveness of the Lord Jesus. Forgiveness demands a kind of death to pettiness, grudges, jealousy and superiority over others. It takes sacrifice to forgive. But forgiveness leads to life. It heals, it brings joy, it initiates new relationships. It leads to a kind of resurrection. Perhaps there is no better way to live the paschal mystery than to forgive as we have been forgiven. It is a sign of love that recalls the reason the Lord came to us: to forgive sin and reunite us with his Father.

WITNESSING TO THE LORD

Living the paschal mystery involves above all else a willingness to witness to the death and resurrection of Jesus Christ and the salvation that has been won for everyone.

How well do you witness to the Lord in both word and deed? Check your performance in these areas. Mark according to this scale:

4 — I do this often
3 — I do this occasionally
2 — I do this rarely
1 — I never do this

____ 1. I speak about my religious beliefs with others.

____ 2. I forgive others when they wrong me.

____ 3. I deny myself small pleasures from time to time.

____ 4. I speak the truth even when it hurts.

____ 5. I try to endure personal setbacks cheerfully; I attempt to find value even in defeat.

____ 6. I make sacrifices for the poor.

____ 7. I help people in need.

____ 8. I speak well of people who are being verbally abused by others.

____ 9. I receive the Eucharist.

____10. I try to participate fully in the Mass.

____11. I thank the Lord for what he has done for me.

____12. I live my life joyfully.

Reflection:

1. List three ways in which you witness to the mystery of God's love in your life:

   a. _____

   _____

   b. _____

   _____

   c. _____

   _____

2. Select one of the items from the 12 points above and resolve to improve your performance this coming month. Check your progress daily, perhaps even recording your thoughts in a diary.

SUMMARY

1. The Last Supper prefigured the sacrifice of the cross when Jesus gave himself to the Father for the redemption of all people.

2. Jesus' trial revealed that his enemies wished to eliminate him because he was a threat to established Jewish beliefs. They presented him as a potential political bother to the Roman authorities.

3. The passion and crucifixion of Jesus show that he freely and obediently gave his life for us. His last words reveal him as a person who died as he lived: forgiving, concerned with others and accepting of his Father's will.

4. Although the resurrection narratives differ in details, they all attest to the same basic reality: The crucified Jesus has arisen from the dead; he has appeared to his friends and disciples; he reigns in glory at the right hand of his Father; he and his Father have sent the Holy Spirit to those who believe.

5. Those theories which tend to deny that Jesus actually rose bodily from the grave generally ignore one or more of the following points:

   a. Jesus was a real, historical person. The claims his disciples made about him make Christianity a unique religion, quite different from the pagan religions of the day.

   b. It is highly unlikely that the early Christians would have been willing to suffer martyrdom for the sake of a story they had created themselves.

   c. The scriptural accounts insist that Jesus was actually seen, that he appeared to his friends, even ate with them.

6. The paschal mystery refers to God's love for us accomplished through the passion, death and resurrection/glorification of Jesus. Jesus passed over to a new life

through his death, conquering both sin and death. What the Father did for him he will do for us through our faith in the living Lord.

7. Christians are daily called to live the death and resurrection of Jesus. They do this by self-denial, love, forgiveness, witnessing to the Lord, and the like.

EXERCISES

Do one of the following:

1. Visit a Catholic cemetery. Find symbols of hope in the resurrection. Report to the class.
2. Research Catholic belief in life after death. Check a Catholic encyclopedia or catechism. Report to the class.
3. Prepare a witness talk on how the living Lord has touched your life.
4. Make a list of ways Jesus can be found in the world today. Illustrate this list through drawings, pictures, symbols, etc.
5. Interview five Catholic adults. Ask what they believe about Jesus' resurrection. Report your findings.

SCRIPTURE REFLECTION

Since you have been brought back to true life with Christ, you must look for the things that are in heaven, where Christ is, sitting at God's right hand. Let your thoughts be on heavenly things, not on the things that are on the earth, because you have died, and now the life you have is hidden with Christ in God. But when Christ is revealed—and he is your life—you too will be revealed in all your glory with him (Col 3:1-4).

SEVEN

Titles of Jesus—
Faith of the Early Church

Jesus and his disciples left for the villages round Caesarea Philippi. On the way he put this question to his disciples, "Who do people say I am?" And they told him. "John the Baptist," they said "others Elijah; others again, one of the prophets." "But you," he asked "who do you say I am?" Peter spoke up and said to him, "You are the Christ." And he gave them strict orders not to tell anyone about him.

—Mark 8:27-30

You can tell a lot about people by the titles and nicknames others give them. For example, you probably expect The Brain to be smart, The Sex Bomb to be physically attractive and The Business Person of the Year to be a financial success.

So it is with Jesus. The early Christians used certain titles when they reflected on Jesus. The New Testament records a number of these. Even Jesus himself often used one of these titles—Son of Man—when referring to himself.

These titles help us understand what Jesus did for us and who he is. They also shed light on what the early Christians believed about our Lord. This chapter will discuss some of these titles.

FAITH SURVEY

Before studying certain titles of Jesus, complete this check list. These statements reflect Christian belief about Jesus. Put the letter of your choice next to each statement. The letter should reflect your current position in regard to the statement.

A — I understand this statement, and I believe it.

B — I believe this statement, but I do not understand it.

C — I am not sure what this statement means.

D — This statement does not reflect my belief.

_____ 1. Jesus is the Son of God.

_____ 2. Jesus is my Lord.

_____ 3. Jesus is fully man.

_____ 4. Jesus is fully God.

_____ 5. Jesus is the Son of Man.

_____ 6. Jesus is the Messiah.

_____ 7. Jesus is my personal savior.

_____ 8. Jesus is the man for others.

_____ 9. Jesus lives!

_____ 10. Jesus is the Second Person of the Blessed Trinity.

For Discussion and Reflection:

1. What do the following titles reveal about the person?

   Buddha, the Enlightened One
   Ivan the Terrible
   Peter the Rock
   Ali, the Great One

   Add some names to this list, especially names of sport and rock personalities. Do the titles really capture the person? Explain.

2. Play the following word association game with at least 10 people, both young and old, believers and nonbelievers.

a. Ask each person to mention the first feeling or idea that comes to mind at the word *Jesus.*

b. Compile a list of the responses. For example, one person might respond, "God," another person may say "love," and so on.

c. In small groups share your findings and divide the responses into two sets:

- words that emphasize *who Jesus is* (his nature)
- words that emphasize *what he does for us* (his function)

  Example: "God" would be put under the first category; "love" could be put under either category

d. Discuss the following questions:

- Do people tend to emphasize what Jesus does rather than who he is? Why or why not?
- When you pray to Jesus, do you tend to praise him for who he is or do you tend to ask him to do things for you? Which is better to do? Explain.
- From what you have read about Jesus in the New Testament, do the evangelists emphasize his function (his saving deeds for us) or his nature (who he is as God's Son)? Or is the emphasis about equal? Give examples.

CHRIST, THE SUFFERING SERVANT

As noted in the first chapter, *Christ* is not a surname. Rather, it is one of the most important titles Christians give to Jesus. Our own designation as followers of Jesus Christ—*Christians*—demonstrates the importance of this title even for our own self-identity.

When dealing with the titles of Jesus, scholars debate the following:

1. Did Jesus himself use the title when talking about himself? And if he did, did he mean by it the same thing his contemporaries did?

2. Did Jesus accept the title, though never using it to refer to himself?
3. Was the title given to Jesus by the early Christians under the guidance of the Holy Spirit?

As we have seen, the gospels are not biographies of Jesus. They are faith summaries written some 35 to 70 years after Jesus' death and resurrection. Thus it is not always easy to sift through the evidence and come up with clear answers to the three questions above.

But we do know one thing for certain: Early Christians most definitely called Jesus the *Christ.* The English word *Christ* comes from the Greek word *Christos. Christos* translates the Hebrew word *Messiah. Messiah* means "anointed one."

Most Jews of our Lord's day believed that the messiah (anointed one) would be a descendent of King David, and would bring God's peace and justice once again to the nation of Israel. But as we have seen, the various Jewish sects had somewhat different ideas of what the messiah would be. For example, the Pharisees expected a religious leader who would fit into their practice of interpreting the Law; the Essenes expected two messiahs, one from a priestly family, another from a kingly family; the Zealots looked for a revolutionary leader who would throw off the yoke of Roman oppression. Even some of the apostles had the notion of an earthly king in mind when they applied the title to Jesus.

Mark's gospel treats the title of Christ in an interesting way. In his gospel we find a certain pattern of concealment of Jesus' identity as the Messiah.

Please read Mark 1:34,44; 3:12; 5:43; 7:36; 8:26,30; 9:9.

What is common to all the verses above is Jesus' reluctance to let his identity be known. In the famous passage quoted at the beginning of this chapter Jesus asked the apostles, "Who do people say I am?" They replied, giving names like John the Baptist, Elijah or some other great prophet. But Jesus asked the direct question of his apostles, "And you, who do you say that I am?"

Peter spoke up for them all and responded with, "You are the Christ!" Strangely, though, Jesus orders Peter not to tell anyone about this identification.

Why would Jesus want his identity as the Messiah kept secret? Again, we can turn to Mark for an answer. Here are the verses immediately following the above exchange with the apostles:

> And he began to teach them that the Son of Man was destined to suffer grievously, to be rejected by the elders and the chief priests and the scribes, and to be put to death, and after three days to rise again; and he said all this quite openly. Then, taking him aside, Peter started to remonstrate with him. But turning and seeing his disciples, he rebuked Peter and said to him, "Get behind me, Satan! Because the way you think is not God's way but man's" (Mk 8: 31-33).

What does this passage reveal? For one thing, note how Jesus began to teach that he would suffer, be rejected by the religious leaders and eventually be put to death only to rise in three days. He taught this immediately after accepting the title of Messiah from Peter. This did not sit well with Peter. How could the Messiah meet rejection, suffering and death? This did not fit the notion of messiah that everyone had, including the apostles. Peter was quite indignant at Jesus' teaching, took him aside and disagreed with him sharply. We can imagine the sharp-tongued, impetuous Peter saying something like this: "What do you mean, you are going to be rejected by the very leaders of our religion? And be put to death? Come on now! Are you feeling all right? Stop talking this nonsense!"

But Jesus was emphatic. He made a point of positioning Peter in front of the apostles and telling him—and through him the others—that he was like the devil himself. Their concept of a messiah was wrong. They imagined him as an earthly king who would usher in a golden age through the use of violence or some flashy miracles. Jesus did not want to be tempted by this false idea. Being an earthly king was an attractive notion, tempting, convenient—but not God's will. Jesus ordered Peter to get

behind him, thus symbolizing an absolute refusal to accept a false notion of messiah.

Why, then, was Jesus reluctant to reveal his messianic identity to people during his lifetime? Simply because they did not understand what he understood by the title Messiah. He did not wish to mislead them. He wanted to give them time to reflect on his person and on his mission for the sake of the kingdom before they rashly ascribed to him titles that reflected their limited understanding.

Not until after the resurrection, ascension and glorification of Jesus did the early Christian community begin to see clearly what he meant by messiahship. His concept was that of a suffering servant, the very opposite of a great political leader.

The title, Suffering Servant, finds its roots in the writings of Second Isaiah, especially in the four Servant Songs. The most famous Suffering Servant Song is found in Isaiah 53. The Servant, with whom Jesus identified himself, was a mysterious, symbolic figure who represented all of Israel and who took upon himself the sins of the people and through suffering atoned for their guilt. You might wish to read the entire song quoted in Isaiah, but please note this passage:

> And yet ours were the sufferings he bore,
> ours the sorrows he carried.
> But we, we thought of him as someone punished,
> struck by God, and brought low.
> Yet he was pierced through for our faults,
> crushed for our sins.
> On him lies a punishment that brings us peace,
> and through his wounds we are healed (Is 53:4-5).

For Jesus, the Messiah was the Suffering Servant. After Easter and the gift of the Holy Spirit on Pentecost, the early Christians came to see that Jesus was the "anointed one" in this sense. They had witnessed his death—a death for the remission of sins—and they had witnessed the resurrection. They saw in Jesus the one who was promised, the representative of Yahweh who established true peace and justice not only for Israel but for all nations. Their understanding of the Messiah underwent transformation from the pre-Easter Jewish interpretations to the post-Easter understanding of Messiah as heavenly king.

To designate Jesus as the Christ (Messiah) is to believe that he is God's anointed one, the one who has come to establish his Father's kingdom on earth, the one who sits at the Father's right hand in heaven, the one who will come at the end of time to judge the living and the dead.

JESUS THE MESSIAH

In our Lord's day most Jews expected a messiah to come and save them. This belief came from Old Testament prophecies. But the prophets had several images of the messiah.

Check the following prophetic references to the messiah. Describe the kind of messiah prophesied.

Isaiah 9:5-7 _____

_____

Isaiah 40:10-11 _____

_____

Isaiah 52:13 _____

Isaiah 53:6-7 _____

Micah 5:1-4 _____

_____

Malachi 3:1-5 _____

_____

Now read one of the following passages from the New Testament about Jesus. Share what you read with your classmates, discussing the various actions and teachings of Jesus which prompted people to think of him as the Messiah.

Matthew 3:13-4:11   Mark 11:1-11
Matthew 11:1-19   Luke 4:16-28
Matthew 17:1-13   John 10:1-21
Mark 2:1-12   John 13:1-20

LORD

Lord is another significant title given to Jesus. During his earthly ministry, various people called Jesus Lord. This address meant something like sir or master. It was a sign of respect. But a lord was also a ruler or owner of land. Jesus was given this title after Pentecost to show that he was Lord of the universe.

Closely associated with the idea of Jesus as ruler of the universe was the belief that only God was Lord of all creation. In fact, when the Hebrew scriptures were translated into the Greek Septuagint version some years before the birth of Jesus, the Jewish scripture scholars used the Greek word *Kyrios* (Lord) to translate the Hebrew word for God, *Yahweh.* Thus, *Lord* means God.

To call Jesus Lord is to affirm that he is God himself. It was the earliest title used after the resurrection to designate the divinity of Jesus, the Christ.

Of all the New Testament writers, St. Paul uses "Lord" the most. Along with "Christ," it is Paul's favorite title for Jesus. He calls Jesus "the Lord," "our Lord," "the Lord Jesus," "our Lord Jesus," "the Lord Jesus Christ," "our Lord Jesus Christ," and "Jesus Christ our Lord." St. Paul proclaims time and again one of the most ancient Christian creeds: Jesus is Lord! We who call Jesus Lord believe that he—a simple carpenter, a wandering preacher, a condemned criminal—is God. This man lives and is real. He is Lord—God.

THE JESUS PRAYER

In recent years many Christians have rediscovered the Jesus Prayer. This prayer has its origins in certain New Testament phrases. The practice of saying the prayer repetitively probably began with the fourth-century hermits of the Egyptian deserts. Christians in the Charismatic Movement have helped to revitalize the prayer, finding in it the power of the Lord's name. It is sometimes said in a group and aloud, but more often silently "in the heart."

The prayer has a variety of forms. One of the most common is:

Lord, Jesus Christ, Son of the Living God,
have mercy on me, a sinner.

The simplest variation of the prayer consists of one word, "Jesus," repeated quietly with love and trust.

SON OF MAN

One of the most mysterious New Testament titles is the one Jesus used in speaking about himself: *Son of Man*. This is the only title Jesus used when referring to himself. In the Aramaic spoken by Jesus, *Son of Man* could simply mean "man." Thus, one of the most popular interpretations of this title is that Jesus was identifying himself very strongly with all people when he called himself the Son of Man. Jesus joins himself to us and identifies himself as one of us.

Scholars have noted, though, that the purely general sense of this title—"man"—does not seem to fit all the gospel texts where it appears. In many texts Jesus seems to speak of the Son of Man as a particular person.

We must turn to the Hebrew scriptures, specifically the Book of Daniel, to solve the riddle of this title. Daniel is an example of apocalyptic literature. An apocalypse is a highly symbolic form of writing which deals with the final period of world history and the catastrophe that will bring about the end of the world. In the final catastrophe the powers of evil will make a supreme struggle against God, but they will be routed after a dreadful and bloody combat. The evil powers, depicted allegorically, are the world kingdoms in power at the time of the writing of the apocalypse. In the final combat, the Jewish nation—sometimes represented with a messiah as leader—triumphs over the world.

In Daniel's apocalypse Daniel has a vision that depicts in highly symbolic language various kingdoms the Jews lived under after losing their independence (see Chapter 2). In a second vision

Daniel sees the kingdoms destroy one another and fall to the dust of the earth. Then he sees, at the end of time,

> "coming on the clouds of heaven,
> one like a son of man" (Dn 7:13).

While the beastly kingdoms destroy themselves, the Son of Man is led before God:

> "On him was conferred sovereignty,
> glory and kingship,
> and men of all peoples, nations and languages
>   became his servants.
> His sovereignty is an eternal sovereignty
> which shall never pass away,
> nor will his empire ever be destroyed" (Dn 7:14).

What significance does this title, Son of Man, have? Jesus seems to have borrowed his imagery from Daniel's apocalypse (and also from two other books which do not appear in the inspired Hebrew writings, the Ethiopic book of Enoch and the fourth book of Esdras). Here the title indicates a saving, ruling role for Jesus. He is the Savior who will come at the end of time to establish God's kingdom for all people.

In many of the 82 sayings in which this title appears, it is linked to the Suffering Servant. Thus it carried connotations of the messiah-like figure of Daniel, but also served Jesus as a good vehicle to identify himself as a Suffering Servant for all of his brothers and sisters.

SON OF GOD

The title *Son of God* has become an important designation for Jesus through the ages. It is rarely used in the synoptic gospels but can be found more frequently in John and Paul. This title certainly reflects the faith of the early Christians—and our faith, too—that Jesus is God-made-flesh. The title lucidly presents who Jesus is in himself and for his followers.

FALSE IMAGES

In his classic book, *Your God Is Too Small,* John B. Phillips writes of certain false ideas of God that tend to make people reject authentic belief in God. It is not that these people do not believe in God, but that their belief is misplaced, that is, based on a false conception of God.

Certain false beliefs about Jesus turn people away from the real Jesus of our faith. In Chapter 3 we mentioned the "Holy Card Jesus" who is depicted as meek and mild, somewhat effeminate and overly pious.

Describe and discuss other false images of Jesus, such as:

Jesus the Superstar

Jesus the Divine Superman

Jesus the Heavenly Security Blanket

How are these images false? Back up your response with a New Testament passage.

WORD OF GOD

One of the loftiest titles bestowed on Jesus by the early church is *Word of God.* The prologue to John's gospel underscores this theme:

In the beginning was the Word:
the Word was with God
and the Word was God.
He was with God in the beginning.
Through him all things came to be,
not one thing had its being but through him.
All that came to be had life in him
and that life was the light of men (Jn 1:1-4).

We don't typically use *Word of God* when we address Jesus in prayer. As a title, *Word of God* is deeply meditative and theological, suggesting a rich reflection on the nature of Jesus.

We turn first to Greek thought to search out a meaning for this title. In Greek philosophy, *Logos* (Word) was the mediating principle between God and his creation. When this title is applied to Christ, Jesus is seen as the mediator between the Father and human beings. He is the perfect example of how people should relate to the almighty God. As St. John so aptly puts it, Jesus is "the Way, the Truth and the Life."

The Hebrew world had a great respect for the word. The Jews considered words to be representations of our thoughts, indeed of our very selves. For example, when I converse with you, I share a part of myself. I present myself to you. In an analogous way, God also speaks in words. For example, creation is a word of God—an expression of himself that tells us something about him. Creation communicates (represents) God's greatness, his power, his grandeur.

God also speaks to us by working in our history. Thus, the Jews heard the call of God's loving mercy as he led them through the desert into the Promised Land. In the Old Testament, God spoke in other ways, too; for example, through the prophets and in worship. The prophets spoke God's word when they called men and women to act more lovingly toward their fellow Jews regardless of age or sex or financial position.

We Christians believe that God still speaks to us today. His word can be found in many places. For example, the Bible is a living word of God addressed to each of us. In addition, God speaks to us in the very depths of our beings and through other people. Prayer, quiet reflection on the events of our lives, silent response to the promptings of our inner voice of conscience—all of these are ways we get in touch with the word of God spoken in our lives.

Though we grant the validity and importance of all these ways through which God speaks to us, we Christians recognize that he spoke uniquely and continues to speak today through his *Word,* his own Son made flesh. Jesus is the Father's perfect Word, his perfect expression. Jesus represents the Father for us. He is the fullest expression of God in created reality. Jesus is God-made-flesh. Words are the flesh of ideas. Jesus (the Word) is God-made-flesh. He is God presented to us in a form that we can see, hear, touch. He is the visible sign of the invisible God.

Reflecting on St. John's theology of the Word, we should note that the Son was instrumental in creating the world, "through him all things came to be." Thus, the Word is the model on whom creation finds its fullest glory; he is the pattern for creation's reconciliation with God. And for us, Jesus is the model to follow on our journey to the Father. The mystery of creation and our own personal existence is found in him.

SYMBOLS OF JESUS

Symbols are signs of reality. Words, for example, are symbols of ideas; they are signs we can see or hear. In a real way Jesus is the perfect symbol of the Father, that is, a visible sign of the invisible God. Christians have often used symbols to communicate their beliefs about Jesus. Here are a few:

The Alpha and Omega. These are the first and last letters of the Greek alphabet. They symbolize that Jesus is the beginning and end of human history. In him we can find the meaning of life.

ΙΧΘΤΣ Fish. ΙΧΘΤΣ in Greek means "fish." It is an anagram for the first letters of a short creed. The creed reads, "Jesus Christ Son of God Savior."

Ι	—Iesous	= Jesus
Χ	—Christos	= Christ
Θ	—Theou	= of God
Τ	—Uios	= Son
Σ	—Soter	= Savior

Sacred Monogram. I and C are the first letters of Jesus Christ in Latin; in Greek, the first syllable of Jesus.

Chi-Rho. Chi and Rho are the first two letters of the Greek word for Christ. This is perhaps the most common symbol for our Lord.

In the space provided, create your own symbol for Jesus. Share this with your classmates.

Reflective Essay. Write a short essay describing a time when the Lord spoke in your life through an event, an experience, a person, etc. Share this faith statement with your friends.

PROPHET, PRIEST, KING

Three traditional titles Christians have given to Jesus are *prophet, priest* and *king.* These titles identify who Jesus is and speak about what he has accomplished for us as our Savior.

Prophet emphasizes Jesus' role as one who testifies to the truth. As Jesus said to Pilate, the truth shall set us free. It takes courage to speak the truth; it is difficult to be a prophet. We saw how Jesus—like many prophets before him—was put to death because the authorities did not want to hear the truth. But the truth Jesus spoke has truly set people free. In this sense he is a liberator; his message leads to quiet inner conversion which frees men and women of their hate, their pride, their preoccupation with money, property, sex and the like.

A *priest* is a mediator between God and his people. He is a go-between. The letter to the Hebrews refers to Jesus as the High Priest:

> "But now Christ has come, as the high priest of all the blessings which were to come. . . . And he has entered the sanctuary once and for all, taking with him not the blood of goats and bull calves, but his own blood, having won an eternal redemption for us" (Heb 9:11-12).

Jesus has united us with his Father, and by his sacrifice he has atoned for our sins, offenses and negligences. He has brought us into union with the source of life.

As *king,* Jesus rules creation at the right hand of his Father. His rule is one of loving service. Recall these powerful words of the Lord right after he performed the lowly task of washing the feet of his apostles at the Last Supper:

> "You call me Master and Lord, and rightly; so I am. If I, then, the Lord and Master, have washed your feet, you should wash each other's feet. I have given you an example so that you may copy what I have done to you" (Jn 13:13-15).

As we have seen in our discussion of Jesus as the Christ, Jesus' rule will be perfectly realized at the end of time when all creation shall recognize him as the Lord of heaven and earth.

By virtue of our baptism we share in the prophetic, priestly and kingly ministry of our Lord Jesus Christ. We are prophets when we proclaim the truth of the gospel; priests when we show through our love and witness that Jesus Christ is the Way to the Father; kings when we serve as Jesus did.

SUMMARY

Each of Jesus' New Testament titles reveals something about his nature and his function as our Savior. Most of the titles stress what Jesus has done (and does) for us rather than who he is; they underscore his role in salvation history. What follows is a list of the important titles of Jesus from the New Testament with a brief statement of the key meaning behind each.

- Christ (Messiah) — the Promised One who brings the kingdom of God; the Anointed One who is the Suffering Servant of God.
- Lord (*Kyrios*) — Jesus is divine; he is God.
- Son of Man — the Suffering Servant who will usher in God's kingdom at the end of time; a man who shares our plight.
- Son of God — the unique Son who is divine.
- Word of God — the total self-communication of the Father.
- Prophet, Priest, King — Jesus' roles as witness to the truth, mediator between God and his people, and servant who is Lord of creation.

EXERCISES

Other Titles of Jesus. What does each of the following titles say about early Christian belief concerning Jesus? Is the title meaningful to you? Explain. Which title is your favorite? Discuss.

- Good Shepherd
  (Jn 10:11)
- Lamb of God
  (Jn 1:29)
- Stone rejected by the
  builders (Acts 4:11)
- Son of Mary (Mk 6:3)

- The last Adam (Rom 5:15-21)
- Judge of the living and the
  dead (Acts 17:31)
- Bread of life (Jn 6:35)
- The Way, the Truth and the
  Life (Jn 14:6)

New Titles of Jesus. If Jesus entered history in the last two decades of this century, what would be some titles his followers might attach to him? You may wish to borrow ideas from the worlds of advertising, politics, movies, music and the like. Explain how each of the titles you use tells something of importance about Jesus.

Being Prophet, Priest, King. All Christians are called on to share in Jesus' ministry of truth (prophet), mediation (priest), and service (king). How about you?

1. As a class construct three lists:

   a. Ways we can serve the truth.
   b. Ways we can bring God to others.
   c. Ways we can serve others.

2. Select something from each list and resolve to act on it this week.

3. Select several other items from each list and evaluate your performance (from *5*—excellent to *1*—poor).

SCRIPTURE REFLECTION

He is the image of the unseen God
and the first-born of all creation,
for in him were created
all things in heaven and on earth:
everything visible and everything invisible,
Thrones, Dominations, Sovereignties, Powers—
all things were created through him and for him.
Before anything was created, he existed,
and he holds all things in unity.
Now the Church is his body,
he is its head.

As he is the Beginning,
he was first to be born from the dead,
so that he should be first in every way;
because God wanted all perfection
to be found in him
and all things to be reconciled through him and
     for him,
everything in heaven and everything on earth,
when he made peace
by his death on the cross (Col 1:15-20).

EIGHT

Belief in Jesus Through the Ages

But the serpent, with his cunning, seduced Eve, and I am afraid that in the same way your ideas may get corrupted and turned away from simple devotion to Christ. Because any newcomer has only to proclaim a new Jesus, different from the one that we preached, or you have only to receive a new spirit, different from the one you have already received, or a new gospel, different from the one you have already accepted—and you welcome it with open arms.
—2 Corinthians 11:3-4

Through the centuries Christians have tried to plumb the depths of the mystery of Jesus Christ, God's sign of his love for his people. For almost 2000 years the church has been a steady guide, helping people to reflect on and understand the story of God's friendship for us in Jesus Christ.

This chapter discusses the response of the church to the question, *Who is Jesus Christ?* It especially focuses on the early centuries of Christianity when much of the philosophical reflection about Jesus was hammered out in the early councils. It will also take up a few questions that people are asking about Jesus today. The following chapter will then discuss certain modern images of Jesus.

171

A SHORT DESCRIPTION

Write a short essay describing your best friend. Try to capture the very essence of the person. Share these descriptions and then discuss the following questions:

a. Can you ever capture your friend in words? Why or why not?

b. Do we need more than the gospels to better understand Jesus? Why or why not?

c. Have your perceptions of Jesus changed since you were a child? If so, how?

d. What questions do you now have about Jesus that you never had before?

THE JESUS OF THE COUNCILS

Catholics believe that God's revelation, his self-communication to us, reached its fullest expression in the person of Jesus Christ. Jesus accomplished our redemption by establishing a new covenant by which we have all been saved.

As we have seen, the early Christians witnessed firsthand the marvelous deeds Jesus accomplished for us. They heard and reflected on his teaching. They saw and marveled at his miracles. They witnessed his death. Most important, they experienced his resurrection, meeting him as one alive with God's full power and in their very midst.

The New Testament writers tell of Jesus' appearances to his friends after his resurrection. But they also record Jesus' return to his Father. Though Jesus returns in full glory to his Father, he does not abandon his disciples. He promised:

"And know that I am with you always; yes, to the end of time" (Mt 28:20).

At the time of his ascension Jesus renewed his promise to send the Holy Spirit to his disciples. Luke records that this took place on Pentecost Sunday. Catholics believe that the Holy Spirit, sent by our Lord and the Father, has remained with the church through the centuries and is alive and active in the world today.

One of the major functions of the Spirit is to guide the Christian community in truth, to aid it in preaching the Father's love for us through his Son. Another major function of the Spirit is to give us Christians the courage to live as Jesus taught us to live. A major way the Spirit of truth helps to keep the good news of Jesus alive is through the *teaching office of the church.* Jesus established this teaching office when he said to Peter:

> "You are Peter and on this rock I will build my Church. And the gates of the underworld can never hold out against it. I will give you the keys of the kingdom of heaven: whatever you bind on earth shall be considered bound in heaven; whatever you loose on earth shall be considered loosed in heaven" (Mt 16:18-19).

This teaching office resides in Peter and his successors, that is, the pope and bishops in union with him. Their task as teachers is to make sure that Christians through the ages don't distort their belief in the good news of Jesus and live contrary to its spirit of love.

The church in the centuries after the apostles was faced with the task of passing on its faith in Jesus. The New Testament writings were (and are) absolutely essential in helping later Christians understand who Jesus is and what he has accomplished for us. We saw in the last chapter, for example, how the titles of Jesus helped the first couple of generations of Christians reflect on Jesus. But beyond the scriptures, a need arose for further development in *Christology,* that is, a need to reflect more deeply on the nature and mission of Jesus Christ.

Why Did Doctrine About Jesus Develop?

Father Richard McBrien observes that the church's understanding of faith developed for three reasons: 1) Men and women are basically inquisitive. They want to know more. They want to understand as best they can who Jesus is. It is natural for them to ask questions and then to pose solutions to them. 2) Doctrine had to develop because some people began to teach things about Jesus which did not go along with what Christians traditionally believed about the Lord. Their heretical (that is, false) teachings confused people and threatened the very faith on which Christianity was established. 3) As Christianity spread, it became necessary to communicate the Christian message across cultural lines. The good news of Jesus had to be preached in a manner in which people could grasp who Jesus was and what he did for us.

These three factors led to development in the church's teaching about Jesus in the first seven centuries or so of Christianity. The second factor in particular forced the church to take stands against certain false teachings which threatened the very heart of Christian belief in Jesus. During this era the greatest *doctrinal* development in teachings about Jesus took place. And it took place in *ecumenical* (that is, worldwide or general) *councils* of the church. The most important of these official church assemblies are listed here:

Council of Nicaea (325)
First Council of Constantinople (381)
Council of Ephesus (431)
Council of Chalcedon (451)
Third Council of Constantinople (680-681)

THE HOLY SPIRIT

St. Paul knew well the importance of the Holy Spirit for the life of the church. The Spirit has bestowed gifts on the members of Christ's body for the purpose of building it up. Paul lists some of these gifts in 1 Corinthians 12. They include preaching with wisdom, instruction, faith, healing, miracles, prophecy, recognizing spirits, speaking in tongues and interpreting tongues. The greatest gift of all, though, is love.

Read 1 Corinthians 12. Try to identify your greatest gift. What is special about you? What quality do you possess that really helps other people experience the good news of Jesus? Here are some possibilities. Check off one that best typifies you. Add to this list if you like. Share your choice with a friend and explain why you chose as you did.

_____ Joyful   _____ Thoughtful

_____ Generous   _____ Helpful

_____ Forgiving   _____ Intelligent

_____ Accepting   _____ Gentle

_____ Courageous   _____ _____

_____ Patient   _____ _____

Discuss: How can each of the qualities listed above build up the
Christian community of your home, parish and school?
Give specific examples.

Jesus—God and Man

The history of doctrinal development concerning Jesus is
fascinating but complex. To follow the raging debates that went
on during these centuries requires a grasp of Greek philosophy
and a sense of history. To simplify, we might say that problems
arose when either Jesus' divinity was so emphasized that his
humanity was denied, or when his humanity was so stressed that
his divinity was ignored or denied.

**The Denial of
Jesus' True Humanity**
One of the first challenges to
apostolic faith in Jesus came from
the Docetists during the first cen-
tury. *Docetism* held that Jesus only seemed to be a man, that
though his body appeared real, it was an illusion, a ghost. This
heresy and another similar to it—*Gnosticism*—taught that
material reality was evil and unimportant. Both heresies could
not accept the fact that God had become man, thus uniting
himself to material reality. It was inconceivable that God could
hunger and thirst, experience fear, suffer and die. So, according
to them, he did not. John's gospel attacks this position when it
insists that the Word of God became *flesh* (Jn 1:14), thus em-
phasizing that Jesus had a real body, like all humans.

What is the danger of Docetism? If Jesus only seemed
human, then he only seemed to die. His resurrection was an illu-

sion. His teachings and miracles and associations with people were not real as we know reality.

If Jesus were not truly a man, then the Bible could hardly say:

> For it is not as if we had a high priest who was incapable of feeling our weaknesses with us; but we have one who has been tempted in every way that we are, though he is without sin (Heb 4:15).

REFLECTION

Find several clear-cut examples from the New Testament which show that the early Christians experienced a truly *human* Jesus, one who had a real human body like us. Share these.

The Denial of Jesus' Divinity The pendulum of belief about Jesus swung to another extreme when a priest by the name of Arius reflected on the meaning of Christ as the Word of God and the Son of God. Arius believed that Jesus was in fact God's Word and Son, but he denied that the Word of God is equal to the Father or that the Son of God always existed. For Arius, Jesus Christ is God's greatest creature, a mediator between God and humans but a creature nonetheless. According to Arius, Jesus is not God-made-man.

This heresy, known as *Arianism,* attracted many adherents and threatened to destroy Christianity itself. Like Docetism, it seriously challenged the heart of our religion. If Jesus is not truly God, by what power and authority does he redeem us from our sins? Our salvation is lost. St. Irenaeus, a great third-century theologian, saw clearly the twin perils of denying either the humanity or divinity of Jesus when he wrote:

> Had he not as a human being overcome our adversary, the enemy would not have been justly overcome. Again, had it not been God who bestowed salvation, we should not have it as a secure possession. And if we had not been united

to God, we could not have become partakers of immortality. For the mediator between God and humankind had to bring both parties into friend-ship and concord through his kinship with both; both to present humankind to God, and make God known to humankind (*Against Heresies,* 3:18.6,7).

The emperor Constantine convened the Council of Nicaea in 325 to deal with the threat of Arius. The Council taught that Jesus Christ was truly God and truly man. The First Council of Constantinople (381) was convened to reaffirm the teaching of Nicaea and to state clearly that Jesus had a human soul. The creed that came from this council (the *Nicene-Constantinopolitan Creed*) is essentially the same profession of faith that we say in our Mass today.

THE NICENE CREED

Prayerfully read this traditional statement of Christian belief, so familiar to all of us:

We believe in one God,
   the Father, the Almighty,
   maker of heaven and earth,
   of all that is seen and unseen.

We believe in one Lord, Jesus Christ,
   the only Son of God,
   eternally begotten of the Father,
   God from God, Light from Light,
   true God from true God,
   begotten, not made, one in Being with the Father.
   Through him all things were made.
   For us men and for our salvation
      he came down from heaven:
   by the power of the Holy Spirit
      he was born of the Virgin Mary, and became man.

For our sake he was crucified under Pontius Pilate;
   he suffered, died, and was buried.
   On the third day he rose again
      in fulfillment of the Scriptures;
   he ascended into heaven
      and is seated at the right hand of the Father.
   He will come again in glory
      to judge the living and the dead,
      and his kingdom will have no end.

We believe in the Holy Spirit, the Lord, the giver of
      life,
   who proceeds from the Father and Son.
   With the Father and the Son he is worshiped and
      glorified.
   He has spoken through the Prophets.
   We believe in one holy catholic and apostolic Church.
   We acknowledge one baptism for the forgiveness of
      sins.
   We look for the resurrection of the dead,
      and the life of the world to come. Amen.

Exercise:

1. Make a list of those phrases in the creed that reflect a belief in the divinity of Jesus.

2. Make a second list of those phrases that argue for a belief in Jesus' humanity.

3. Write your own creed. State what you believe about Jesus Christ at this point in your life. Use titles that are most significant to you. Share your creed with your classmates and be prepared to defend it.

Jesus: One Divine Person With Two Natures

After the Council of Nicaea, the next major debate concerning Jesus dealt with the manner in which he is both God and man at the same time. Of course, this is fundamentally a mystery; we can never fully grasp it.

In trying to understand the mystery of Jesus as God and man, though, some people in the century or so after Nicaea made some fundamental errors. For example, the patriarch of Constantinople, Nestorius, taught that in Christ there were two distinct persons—one divine, the other human. As a result, he thought it was wrong to say that Mary was the mother of the divine person. The Council of Ephesus (431), adopting the view of St. Cyril, condemned Nestorius' view. It taught that Jesus Christ is *one* person—a divine person—and thus it is appropriate to call Mary the mother of God. We worship *one* Christ and Lord, not a human being along with the Word.

A different error was made by Eutyches. He maintained that Jesus' human nature was absorbed into his divine nature. Thus, Eutyches and his followers taught that there is but one nature (*monophysitism* in the Greek) in Christ, a divine nature.

The Council of Chalcedon (451) reaffirmed the teaching of the previous councils and also settled the question of Christ's nature:

> We unanimously teach that the Son, our Lord Jesus Christ, is one and the same, the same perfect in divinity, the same perfect in humanity, true God and true man, consisting of a rational soul and body, consubstantial with the Father in divinity and consubstantial with us in humanity . . . in two natures unconfused, unchangeable, undivided and inseparable. The difference of natures will never be abolished by their being united, but

> rather the properties of each remain unimpaired, both coming together in one person and substance, not parted or divided among two persons, but in one and the same only begotten Son, the Divine Word, the Lord Jesus Christ.

This profession of faith, known as the Chalcedon formula, is the church's classic expression of faith in the person of Jesus Christ. A later council, the Second Council of Constantinople (553), confirmed Chalcedon's teaching while the Third Council of Constantinople (680-681) taught that since Christ had two natures, he also possessed two wills and that Jesus' human will, though distinct from his divine will, is not opposed to it.

The Meaning of Conciliar Teaching   What does it mean to believe in Jesus as a divine person possessing both a divine nature and a human nature? First, when we call Jesus a *person* we are fundamentally identifying *who* he is. Jesus Christ is the person we call the Son of God or the Word of God or the Second Person of the Trinity. There is only one *who* in Jesus.

When we say Jesus possesses two natures, we are addressing the *what* question. Nature concerns what something is and how it acts. A human nature, for example, involves a particular way of being. To be human—to have a human nature—means to have a body and a soul. Humans are different from animals and angels. We exist in a certain way.

Jesus is a divine person who has two natures. What this means is that Jesus is one person who has the nature of being human and the nature of being divine. No one else exists this way. Jesus is absolutely unique. In Jesus God truly becomes *what man is* while remaining *what God is*; Jesus is God-made-man. Thus we can conclude the following:

- God became man, assuming a human body. (To have a human nature means to have a real body.) He was born of Mary, his mother, the mother of God.
- In becoming man Jesus assumed not only a human body but a human soul with intellect and will. Thus Christ had a divine and human mind, a divine and human will.

- The two natures in Christ Jesus are united in one person, the Second Person of the Trinity.
- In becoming man, Jesus Christ remains God. He is God-made-man.
- Our salvation is accomplished through the life, death and resurrection of the *God-man,* Jesus Christ.

DEFENDING THE FAITH

Based on your knowledge of the church's teaching about Jesus, check those statements which clearly distort true belief about Jesus.

_____As a child, Jesus was able to work calculus problems.

_____Jesus was without sin.

_____God did not die on a cross; only the man Jesus did.

_____Jesus experienced the same emotions that we do.

_____Jesus did not suffer pain the way we do.

Discuss:

1. Defend the choices you made in the exercise above.

2. Comment on this quotation from the writings of Dietrich Bonhoeffer, a famous Protestant theologian who died for his faith in a Nazi concentration camp: "If Jesus Christ is not true God, how could he help us? If he is not true man, how could he help us?"

The Pendulum of Belief. The twin dangers of Docetism and Arianism have been with Christians down through the centuries. At times Christians have so emphasized the divinity of Jesus that they have virtually forgotten about his humanity. At other times Christians have so stressed the humanity of Jesus that his divinity is called into question. True belief in Jesus reflects the mystery that Jesus is both truly God and truly man.

Outline a talk entitled "Who Is Jesus Christ?" which you might give to one of the following:

- a 10-year-old child
- a 50-year-old adult
- a teen-age Hindu enrolled at your school as an exchange student from India

Be sure your talk reflects Catholic belief about Jesus.

SOME CONTEMPORARY QUESTIONS

The teaching of the early church councils has greatly influenced theological reflection on Jesus ever since. There has been no doctrinal development since the Third Council of Constantinople; later councils have repeated what the earlier ecumenical councils taught.

Each era of church history has looked to these classic teachings to help answer current questions about Jesus. Here are a few questions that arise in our own day.

How Much Did Jesus Know?

Did Jesus have to learn? More important, did he always know that he was God's Son? These questions try to understand the relationship between the divine nature and the human nature of Jesus. People of our age are concerned with these questions because they want to relate to a *human* Jesus, one who was like us in everything but sin, one who experienced life as we do with all of its uncertainties and risks.

One way to grapple with these questions is to see how previous generations of Christians have answered them. For example, medieval theology held that Jesus had three kinds of knowledge: *beatific knowledge,* that is, God's knowledge of all things; *infused knowledge,* that is, knowledge which requires no learning; and *experimental knowledge,* that is, information gained by living a human life. In our own century, Pope Pius XII taught in an important encyclical that Jesus had the beatific vision "from the time He was received into the womb of the Mother of God." This means that from the moment of conception Jesus knew what God knows, including the fact that he was God.

This approach to the question of Jesus' knowledge settles the issue for many Catholics. But others, in their attempt to understand the knowledge of Jesus, look at certain New Testament passages about Jesus. These passages seem to indicate that in his humanity Jesus did not know everything. For example, when questioned about the end of the world, Jesus says:

> "But as for that day or hour, *nobody* knows it,
> neither the angels of heaven, *nor the Son*; no one
> but the Father" (Mk 13:32, italics added).

Other passages reflect early Christian belief in the humanity of Jesus:

> His state was divine,
> yet he did not cling
> to his equality with God
> but emptied himself
> to assume the condition of a slave,
> and became as men are (Phil 2:6-7).

To be truly human means to grow in knowledge through interaction with one's environment. St. Cyril of Alexandria, an important church Father whose teachings about Jesus greatly influenced the bishops at the Council of Ephesus (431), wrote:

> We have admired his goodness in that for love of
> us he has not refused to descend to such a low
> position as to bear all that belongs to our nature,
> included in which is ignorance.

Modern theologians like Karl Rahner propose the following: First, we must always hold firm to the conviction that Jesus was God from the moment of conception. Regardless of how we answer the question of Jesus' knowledge, we must never claim that he slowly became God. The constant teaching of the New Testament and the Catholic church is that Jesus was always God.

Second, Father Rahner suggests that we distinguish among several kinds of knowledge. There is *intuitive* knowledge which lies at the core of a person's being. You intuitively know that you exist, that you are real, that you are male or female. Then there is *objective* knowledge, the kind you display when you consciously reflect on something. How much is 3 + 3? You know that answer because you have been taught it, and you can reflect on it. You learned it. You have learned many facts which you can think about and reflect on. You have gained objective knowledge.

One way to deal with the question of Jesus' self-knowledge is to say that in the core of his being he always *intuitively* knew he was God's Son. But through his interactions with others, in his prayer, in his reading of scripture and the like, this intuitive knowledge surfaced and became objective knowledge, knowledge he could consciously reflect on.

Thus, in a certain sense, we can say that Jesus grew in knowledge. Like us, he had to gain knowledge of his environment; as Luke says, "Jesus increased in wisdom, in stature, and in favor with God and men" (Lk 2:52).

For many people questions about Jesus' knowledge are not an issue. They look at the New Testament and see that it certainly wasn't of concern to the early Christians. When we encounter the Jesus of the New Testament, that is, when we see Jesus in his public life, we see a Jesus who has an absolutely firm conviction of who he is. He has come to announce God's kingdom and knows that the kingdom is related to his own person and ministry. He reveals God as his Abba. He acts with a sense of mission and conviction which clearly reveal that he knew who he was—the Son of God who has come to save humanity.

FOR DISCUSSION

How do you stand on this question of Jesus' knowledge? Does it help your faith to say that Jesus grew in knowledge? Discuss your reasons with your classmates.

Did Jesus Have Brothers and Sisters?

This question has arisen as more people read the New Testament. There are a few places in the New Testament where reference is made to "brothers and sisters" of Jesus. The most notable example, perhaps, is in Mark's gospel when Jesus returns to his own hometown of Nazareth to announce the coming of God's kingdom:

> They said, "Where did the man get all this? What is this wisdom that has been granted him, and these miracles that are worked through him? This

is the carpenter, surely, the son of Mary, the brother of James and Joset and Jude and Simon. His sisters, too, are they not here with us?" (Mk 6:2-3).

Some Protestant scholars have found no problem in saying that Jesus had blood brothers and sisters. This belief would tend to underscore the humanity of Jesus and his continuity with us.

From the earliest centuries, though, Catholics have maintained that Jesus was born of the virgin Mary and that she always remained a virgin. The gospels of Matthew and Luke support this tradition in their birth narratives concerning Jesus. Their concern is to show that Jesus is both God (conceived by the power of the Holy Spirit) and man (born of Mary). Catholics have traditionally believed in the lifelong virginity of Mary as a sign of her exclusive dedication to the will of God as manifested in her son Jesus Christ.

Scripture scholars have demonstrated that the Greek word for brother, *adelphos,* can also mean "relative" or "kinsman." Thus, traditional Catholic teaching is perfectly reasonable. Jesus did not have blood brothers, but he did have close relatives who, as Mark tells us, grew up in Nazareth with him.

The Jews and the Death of Jesus

A sad part of Christian history has been the attitude that the Jews ought to be held responsible for their rejection of the Messiah. This attitude, found already in Matthew's gospel (Mt 27:25) written around A.D. 80 and repeated by some of the early church Fathers, has been used to justify the prejudice and the many atrocities committed against the Jews throughout the centuries.

In the Middle Ages the Jews suffered severely at the hands of their Christian neighbors: The Black Death, for example, was blamed on the Jewish people and horrible reprisals were enacted against them; at times they were forbidden to marry, to beget children, to practice their religion, to own property, to be seen in public during Holy Week, to engage in certain professions.

In our own century Hitler attempted to annihilate the Jewish people in Europe. He pointed out that his anti-Semitism and "final solution" advocated nothing that had not had church sanction for 800 years. It is certainly true that the Holocaust could never have happened had Christians been unwilling to tolerate it.

This question of Jewish guilt has been an intense issue of the 20th century, particularly in the wake of the Holocaust. The church clearly withdrew any theological basis for anti-Semitism when the church fathers at Vatican II spoke out in emphatic rejection of Jewish responsibility for Jesus' death:

> What happened in His passion cannot be blamed upon all the Jews then living, without distinction, nor upon the Jews of today. . . . The Jews should not be presented as repudiated or cursed by God. . . .
> The Church . . . deplores the hatred, persecutions, and displays of anti-Semitism directed against the Jews at any time and from any source (*Declaration on the Relationship of the Church to Non-Christian Religions*, No. 4).

Anti-Semitism is thoroughly against everything that Jesus stood for. True followers of Jesus Christ abhor prejudice in any form. Christians know that sin brought about Jesus' death—the sin of all people from all times. Jesus accepted his violent death freely in order to redeem all members of the human family.

PREJUDICE

Reflecting on Jesus helps us combat the tendency to judge others as less worthy than ourselves. When God became man in Jesus, he took all of humanity to himself. He loves all people. Christians know that to love God means to love the neighbor in whom God dwells.

Examine how loving you are by marking the following. Then discuss the questions which follow.

Am I someone who . . .

1. is offended when someone says, "I got Jew'd"?   Yes   No   ?

2. believes it is wrong to make ethnic jokes?   Yes   No   ?

3. believes it is wrong to laugh at ethnic jokes?   Yes   No   ?

4. would approve of interracial marriage?   Yes   No   ?

5. who defends people who are victimized by prejudice?   Yes   No   ?

6. befriends people regardless of what others may think?   Yes   No   ?

7. would confess a sin of prejudice?   Yes   No   ?

Discuss:

1. In your judgment, what is the worst form of prejudice in your school? What can you do about it?

2. Is there evidence of prejudice against Jews today in our country? Explain. Is there prejudice against other groups?

3. Offer reasons why prejudice is contrary to who Jesus is and what he taught and did for us.

SUMMARY

1. The teaching office of the church has had to defend true belief in Jesus against misinterpretations.

2. Doctrine about Jesus developed because people are inquisitive, to correct false teaching, and because there was a need to communicate the Christian message across cultural lines.

3. The chart on the following page summarizes the conciliar teaching about Jesus.

HERESY	HERETICAL TEACHING	COUNCIL'S TEACHING
Arianism	Jesus was a creature, not equal to the Father (not divine).	Council of Nicea, 325: Jesus is consubstantial with the Father; he is divine.
Nestorianism	Jesus was two persons —one human, one divine. Mary was only the mother of the human Jesus.	Council of Ephesus, 431: Mary is the mother of God. Jesus is one person, a divine person.
Doceticism	Jesus' body was only an illusion. God could not accept the limitations of being human.	Council of Chalcedon, 451: Jesus is both human and divine.
Monophysitism	Jesus has only one nature, a divine nature (not human).	Council of Chalcedon, 451: Jesus has two natures, one human and one divine.

4. It is possible that the human Jesus had to grow in knowledge.

5. The so-called brothers and sisters of Jesus were his close relatives, his kinsmen.

6. The church condemns anti-Semitism. The Jews as a people are not responsible for the death of Jesus, a death Jesus freely embraced for the remission of the sin of all people.

EXERCISE

As a class, create a questionnaire to survey beliefs about Jesus. Administer it to a representative group of Catholics. Compile the results and then discuss these questions:

1. Do the people you surveyed generally believe what you and your classmates do? Why or why not?

2. Do the people you surveyed accept the teachings of the church about Jesus?

Here are some sample items for your survey:

Instructions: Mark the following statements true (*T*), false (*F*), or don't know (*DK*).

_____ 1. Jesus knew everything even as a child.

_____ 2. Jesus was a sexual being.

_____ 3. Jesus may have looked like a man, but he was really just God.

_____ 4. Jesus is both God and man.

_____ 5. Jesus lives today.

SCRIPTURE REFLECTION

"I am the bread of life.
He who comes to me will never be hungry;
he who believes in me will never thirst.
But, as I have told you,
you can see me and still you do not believe.
All that the Father gives me will come to me,
and whoever comes to me
I shall not turn him away;
because I have come from heaven,
not to do my own will,
but to do the will of the one who sent me" (Jn 6:35-38).

From the movie *Godspell*

NINE

Contemporary Images of Jesus

Day by day
Day by day
Oh, dear Lord, three things I pray:
To see thee more clearly
Love thee more dearly
Follow thee more nearly
Day by day.

—Godspell

Jesus is the Lord of history; his message is timeless. His invitation to respond to God's kingdom touches people of every generation.

People through the ages have reflected on Jesus and his message. They have typically interpreted the meaning of Jesus according to their own needs. They have pictured Jesus as a Jesus for them, a Jesus for their times as well as a Jesus for the ages.

This chapter will focus on how contemporary people have seen Jesus. How have they responded to the question Jesus put to Peter: "Who do people say I am?" (Mk 8:27). We will look first at how today's theologians are picturing Jesus. We will then turn to the media. Finally, we will take a brief look at how some cults present Jesus.

A CONTEMPORARY JESUS

Christians must present anew the person and message of Jesus for each generation. How should this be done? What should be emphasized when presenting Jesus? Reflect on the following and then discuss your choices.

_____ 1. If you had the talent and money, which medium would you choose to tell people today about Jesus?

    a. a successful and popular song

    b. a Hollywood movie

    c. a novel

    d. a play

    e. other:_____

_____ 2. To which group today should the church make a special effort to present the good news of Jesus?

    a. those who support abortion

    b. leaders of dictatorial governments

    c. backers of the arms race

    d. the poor everywhere

    e. other:_____

_____ 3. Of the images that follow, which should be the one given most attention in the church's effort to preach Jesus to others:

    a. Jesus the Liberator

    b. Jesus the Clown

    c. Jesus Christ Superstar

    d. Jesus the Man for Others

    e. other:_____

_____ 4. Let's say you have been given the opportunity to share your faith with a person your own age. The person seems keenly interested in Jesus. You don't want this interest to die. What would you do next?

    a. Invite the person to dinner to discuss more deeply the message of Jesus

    b. Invite the person to read the Bible and pray with you

    c. Introduce the person to Father_____ for instructions in the faith

d. Invite the person to come to Sunday Mass

e. other:_____

Discuss: Share your choices and give the reasons for them.

CONTEMPORARY THEOLOGY LOOKS AT JESUS

In his book *Models of Jesus,* Father John F. O'Grady synthesizes the main images of Jesus discussed by theologians today. Here are a few that are helpful to today's believers:

1. *Jesus — Man for Others.* This view of Jesus concentrates on his loving function of restoring and reconciling people to his Father. Jesus lives not for himself but for all people regardless of their background. Jesus continues today to live in the church, his body. Thus, the living Lord Jesus can be found in the Christian community where he continues his work of reconciliation and restoration.

2. *Jesus — Personal Savior and Healer.* This image of Jesus presents him as the healer of the soul, the spiritual dimension of human life. He came to save people from their sins and to help them overcome their evil ways. This image of Jesus is popular with television preachers and in the charismatic movement where Jesus is seen as healer of physical and psychological ills as well as spiritual ills. Believers expect God to continue to work miracles through his Son Jesus.

3. *Jesus — Clue to the Cosmos, Human Face of God.* Jesus is the answer to our most basic questions about the meaning of life, creation, the nature of God and the nature of what it means to be human. He is the picture in the empty picture frame of creation. He is the Lord and Christ of the world—the one person who can command our highest loyalty. At the same time, by studying how Jesus lived, we will discover what it means to be a human being. He is the model for us to follow.

4. *Jesus — Liberator.* Many people in today's world suffer

political, social and economic oppression. Thousands of people die of starvation every day. Millions of people are forbidden to worship freely or to express themselves without fear of reprisals. More than half the world lives under dictatorships which crush the human spirit. To many people who are suffering, Jesus represents freedom. They see him as one who preached the advent of God's kingdom and who now abides in his followers to help them bring about the fullness of God's kingdom. This kingdom works for the freedom of everyone, freedom from hunger and from every other kind of oppression.

YOUR IMAGE OF JESUS

Which of the images discussed above presents best the Jesus that you know? Give reasons for your choice.

THE JESUS OF POP CULTURE

The popular culture of a people, including the way Jesus is presented, tells a lot about the society itself. Our society, for example, emphasizes a very human Jesus. Two popular musicals of the 1970s are excellent examples: *Jesus Christ, Superstar* and *Godspell.*

The Jesus of *Jesus Christ, Superstar* is a man with feeling—a man who can cry, who needs companionship, who demonstrates impatience. He is an angry Jesus who conveys his teaching in anguished songs appropriate to the rock lyrics of the early 1970s. He is anything but a plastic Jesus.

The Jesus of *Godspell,* a sprightly musical based on Matthew's gospel, is a clown who dances and sings his way through the streets of Manhattan. *Godspell* depicts a joyful, bouncy, cheerful, "street" Jesus. As a clown, Jesus makes us laugh, especially at the pantomimed renditions of the parables, but there is a streak of sadness in his character and he dies victim to an impersonal evil force.

Both *Jesus Christ, Superstar* and *Godspell* give us a very human Jesus. Some art of the past presented a very divine Christ. We can't fault the works for that. But we can point out that they reflect their times; the current emphasis stresses the humanity of Jesus so much that his divinity seems called into question. These contemporary presentations offer a Jesus that appeals to us, but we do not find the real Jesus. They leave out the essence of Christian faith in Jesus—that Jesus is Lord. Although they help us relate to a human Jesus, thus counteracting a previous tendency to view him as a rather plastic figure, they fail to do justice to the gospel portrait of Jesus or to the beliefs of Christians through the ages. They identify Jesus with his teachings on love. But Jesus *is* the love he came to preach. And he lives on. As St. Paul says in 1 Corinthians, if we do not affirm the resurrection of Jesus, we are the most pitiable of people because our faith is in vain.

From the movie *Jesus Christ, Superstar*

A HUMAN JESUS

Obtain the record, libretto or film version of *Jesus Christ, Superstar* or *Godspell.* Listen, view and/or read. Then, discuss the following:

1. Did you like the work? Why or why not?
2. List 10 ways in which the creators of the work emphasize Jesus' humanity.
3. Write a short essay agreeing or disagreeing with the analysis of these contemporary works given above.

Movies, too, have attempted to portray Jesus. These efforts also tend to say more about filmmakers and the paying public than about the historical Jesus. Here are some films, produced in the 1960s, which have received notice.

King of Kings is a remake of Cecil B. DeMille's earlier classic. It depicts a handsome, blond, blue-eyed Jesus who was used as a pawn by the Zealots to overthrow the Romans. *The Greatest Story Ever Told* portrays a squeaky-clean Jesus who speaks in the majestic tones of a Shakespearean actor. The highpoint of the film is the raising of Lazarus to the stirring background of Handel's famous "Hallelujah Chorus." Finally, an interesting portrayal of Jesus appears in Pier Pasolini's *The Gospel According to Saint Matthew.* Pasolini, who discovered and read a copy of the New Testament in his hotel room, attempted to make an objective film version of one of the gospels. Though he succeeded at creating a "you-are-there" flavor in his film, Jesus comes off more as a fiery-eyed communist cell organizer than as our Savior. He rarely smiles and seems consumed with an inner vision that he finds somewhat difficult to express to others.

The 1970s produced perhaps the finest film version of Jesus yet recorded: Zeffirelli's *Jesus of Nazareth.* This made-for-TV movie runs for over six hours. The critics have acclaimed it as the most accurate gospel-based version of Jesus on film. It does indeed seem to present a portrait faithful to what we know of the historical times. The actor who played Jesus in the film has been quoted as saying the part transformed him and made him more religious. Many people who have seen this film have also been moved by it.

Another film, *Jesus,* is based on Luke's gospel. This film is extremely faithful to the text of Luke and presents a reverent, traditional view of Jesus.

The 1980s have not yet produced any notable films on Jesus, though some of the movies of this decade have religious overtones. Some people see images of Jesus in the films listed below. However, these images are essentially false.

- *Superman*—Jesus was not a "man of steel" or "a visitor from another planet." He is not an outsider, but very much one of us.

- The *Star Wars* films—Some people see an appealing theology in the concept of "the Force." But this impersonal force is composed of both good and evil. We know, because Jesus revealed it to us, that the ultimate force in the universe is a benevolent, loving Abba who meets us in prayer, the sacraments, scripture, other people and the like.

- *E.T.*—There are certainly echoes of Christ in E.T.: He is gentle, endowed with supernatural powers, comes back to life, promises when going "home" to also remain with Elliott always. But basically *E.T.* is a delightful fairy tale; we do not find the real Jesus Christ. Jesus is not an alien in the land of humanity. He is God-made-man, both our brother and our God. His coming was no accident; he came to redeem us by his death and resurrection.

JESUS IN TODAY'S FILMS

Discuss the films listed above, and any others in which you see an image of Jesus. Is the image true or false? Does it say something about the real Jesus? or does it merely say something about our society?

Reflect: How much of your image of Jesus comes from the media? Discuss your response with your classmates.

Finally, the music of an age reflects its concerns about almost any issue—love, war and peace, social and economic matters, life and death. To judge from the popular music of the past 25 years or so, we would have to conclude that Jesus and religious questions have had their part to play in the midst of the turbulent musical development from primitive rock to the more sophisticated sounds of today. As *The Rock Music Source Book* puts it:

> Rock has been highly critical of organized religion, and yet it contains many moving statements of faith, cries for help and forgiveness, prayers of praise and thanksgiving to God in general, and to Jesus Christ in particular.

JESUS IN MUSIC

1. Bring in and listen in class to some songs which refer to Jesus from the following categories:
   - soul music
   - country/gospel
   - traditional hymns
   - classical music (like Handel's *Messiah*)
   - rock
   - folk

   a. What do these songs have in common? What are their differences?

   b. What attitudes to Jesus come through—anger, respect, joy, reverence, impatience, etc.?

   c. Which song best reflects your faith in Jesus?

2. Create five song titles about Jesus that would speak meaningfully to your peers about Jesus, for example, "Jesus, Love Me Forever."

   Optional: Write the lyrics for one of these songs. Be sure to share these.

3. Find the lyrics to three songs that depict anti-Christian values. Discuss these with your classmates.

THE JESUS OF THE CULTS

Cults are a phenomenon of our contemporary world. Young people who are disillusioned with the institutional church and yearn for the security an authoritarian structure can provide sometimes fall victim to the cults.

What is a cult? By definition, a cult is a religious group which significantly differs in either belief or practice from one of the major religious groups which are the norm for religious expression in our culture. This sounds harmless enough, but membership in some of these cults has resulted in problems for recruits—neurosis, psychosis, identity confusion, loss of free will, diminished capacity for judgment, alienation from family, false guilt and a host of other undesirable outcomes.

The news media have given increasing attention to the coercive techniques used by some of the cults to gain members. Modern cults often seek out lonely, indecisive and disappointed young people. They offer free invitations to lectures, free meals, workshops or weekend retreats. A favorite technique to win converts is "love bombing," that is, the giving of physical affection and constant attention so the potential member feels accepted and part of the new group.

Once the inductee is hooked, a spate of other techniques are used by some of the cults. Long, confusing lectures are given. This can lead to doctrinal confusion where new truths are accepted on faith because they are too difficult to think through. Some ex-cultists report the widespread practice of diets which deprive the body of essential nutrients and lead to disorientation and emotional susceptibility.

Cult practices also include absolute loyalty, chanting and meditation that discourage objective thinking, extreme conformity, induced hypnotic states, isolation from friends and family, peer pressure by other cult members, unquestioned submission and the like.

All cults have one thing in common: They teach unorthodox doctrines about Jesus. Their teachings fly in the face of the biblical portrait of Jesus, the teaching of the early councils, and the beliefs of Catholics and the main Protestant denominations down through the centuries. For example, some cults teach that Jesus was a created being. This is the view of the Mormons and the Jehovah's Witnesses. The Jehovah's Witnesses teach that Jesus was the incarnation of Michael the Archangel who was created by God (Jehovah). The Way International denies the doctrine of the Trinity and both Christ's divinity and incarnation.

A cult that has received much unfavorable publicity is the Unification Church of Rev. Sun Myung Moon. Like many other cults, the Unification Church tries to gain support for its teachings by making references to Jesus. But Rev. Moon's church is anything but Christian. Many former Moonies testify to the techniques catalogued above, charging that the cult virtually hypnotizes its young adherents by a strict work and dietary regime that keeps them docile and easily led.

Moon's teachings are quite unorthodox. He teaches that God attempted to start a perfect human family with the creation of Adam. But Eve was sexually seduced by Satan and God's attempt to create a perfect race was thwarted. Moon believes that God attempted a second time to create a perfect race through Jesus of Nazareth who was the illegitimate child of Zechariah and Mary. But before Jesus could find his perfect bride, he was killed by the Jews. Moon teaches that a third attempt at creating the perfect human offspring will happen soon. He believes that the new Adam (Messiah) has already been born. Many of the Moonies believe that Moon himself is the new Messiah and his fourth wife the new Eve.

Other cults teach the Hindu belief that there are many revelations (or *avatars*) of God, Jesus being merely one of them. Some of these cults maintain that their current leader is one such *avatar,* equal or sometimes superior to Jesus Christ. Still others maintain that Jesus was a human being who achieved "Christ Consciousness," something everyone can do by following the teachings of the particular cult.

Many cult practices and techniques for gaining members are dangerous. Their teachings about Jesus and many other Christian doctrines not discussed here contradict 2,000 years of traditional Christian beliefs. Their current appeal has resulted from the disorientation of our modern life, people's real search for meaning, dehumanization created by an increasingly technological world, the drug culture, fear of the future and many other factors. We should all respect the beliefs of others, but we must unmask false principles behind the cults.

THE CULTS

Research one of the cults popular today. What does it believe about Jesus? Where does it get its belief? Some possibilities:

Bahais	Jehovah's Witnesses
Christian Science	Rosicrucians
Children of God	Unification Church
Church of Jesus Christ of Latter-day Saints (Mormons)	Way International

For Discussion:

1. What attitude do these groups have toward the Bible? Do they accept it or do they rewrite it to suit their doctrines?

2. Is there something attractive in this cult (religion) that helps explain its popularity with some people?

3. Do these groups affirm both the humanity and divinity of Jesus?

4. What would you do and say if a cult tried to recruit you? Discuss this as a class.

Optional: You may want to read Flo Conway's and Jim Siegelman's *Snapping* (Philadelphia: J. B. Lippincott Co., 1978) to gain a view of how the cults affect personality.

SUMMARY

1. Jesus is universal. His mesage is timeless; it is for people of every generation.

2. Popular contemporary theological images of Jesus include: Man for Others; Personal Savior and Healer; Clue to the Cosmos and Human Face of God; Liberator.

3. The popular culture of a people reveals their beliefs about Jesus. In general, the popular art forms of today stress the humanity of Jesus more than his divinity.

4. The contemporary cults manifest the modern world's quest for meaning. Their teachings about Jesus are unorthodox; they ignore biblical teaching and the constant faith of the church.

EXERCISES

1. Bumper stickers are another indication of popular belief in Jesus. As a class, make a list of Jesus bumper stickers, for example, "Honk if you love Jesus." Do these amuse you? Turn you off? Rekindle your faith?

   Why do people display bumper stickers about Jesus? Why do they wear buttons and other religious symbols? Are these people sincere?

2. Mohandas K. Gandhi has become one of the heroes of the 1980s. He is quoted as saying, "There are so many hungry people in the world that God cannot appear to them except in the form of bread." If Jesus is indeed the Bread of Life and living in his body, the church (the community of Christians), what are some concrete implications of his quote for us?

   As a class, devise a project to help feed the hungry. Be Christ for others by responding to the "least of these."

3. Put together a Christian music festival. Include hymns, Gregorian chant, pieces like Handel's *Messiah*, contemporary Christian rock songs, and so forth.

4. Watch several TV preachers. Compare and contrast their views of Jesus and report to the class.

SCRIPTURE REFLECTION

Your mind must be renewed by a spiritual revolution so that you can put on the new self that has been created in God's way, in the goodness and holiness of the truth.

So from now on, there must be no more lies: *You must speak the truth to one another,* since we are all parts of one another. *Even if you are angry, you must not sin:* never let the sun set on your anger or else you will give the devil a foothold. Anyone who was a thief must stop stealing; he should try to find some useful manual work instead, and be able to do some good by helping others that are in need. Guard against foul talk; let your words be for the improvement of others, as occasion offers, and do good to your listeners. . . . Never have grudges against others, or lose your temper, or raise your voice to anybody, or call each other names, or allow any sort of spitefulness. Be friends with one another, and kind, forgiving each other as readily as God forgave you in Christ (Eph 4:23-32).

TEN

Meeting Jesus Today

"I tell you solemnly once again, if two of you on earth agree to ask anything at all, it will be granted to you by my Father in heaven. For where two or three meet in my name, I shall be there with them."

—Matthew 18:19-20

Jesus invites us to come to him and be both his friend and his disciple. Certainly the payoff is great. What harm can come to us with Jesus as our friend?

Jesus cares about us. He could never abandon us. How are we then to respond to the Lord? What are we supposed to do? Where do we hear him calling to us today? Where do we meet him? What does he ask of us?

We turn to these questions in this chapter.

SELF-EXAMINATION

Anything of value takes work. Excellent students must study hard. They must cultivate the intellectual life. Outstanding athletes must train hard. They must continually work at being in physical condition. Likewise, those of us who aspire to befriend and follow Jesus must cultivate the spiritual life.

Respond to these questions. You may want to share your answers and reasons with a friend.

1. The most spiritual person I know is

   _____

2. For me, *spirituality* means (check three):
   _____ forgiving others
   _____ going to Mass
   _____ giving money to the poor
   _____ reading scripture
   _____ telling others about Jesus
   _____ obeying parents and others in authority
   _____ doing volunteer work
   _____ praying regularly
   _____ living as morally as possible

   _____ (add your own) _____

3. For me, praying is:
   _____ always difficult
   _____ sometimes difficult
   _____ usually easy
   _____ easy

4. If I decided to get closer to the Lord, I would definitely (check two):
   _____ set aside time for personal prayer
   _____ go on a retreat
   _____ help out at home more
   _____ stop indulging every passing whim
   _____ be more careful with my language
   _____ go to Mass and receive communion more often
   _____ do something to help others
   _____ celebrate the sacrament of reconciliation
   _____ read the Bible more
   _____ cut down on some of my weekend activities
   _____ go out of my way to befriend someone who needs a friend

   _____ (other) _____

What does Jesus require of us? Does he expect the kind of response he got from Peter and Andrew and James and John when they dropped their fishing nets and answered his call to follow him? Are we to drop what we are doing and leave everything behind to follow Jesus?

Probably not. What our Lord seeks above all is faith. He wants us to believe deeply that he is alive and active in the world. He wants us to know in our hearts that we are loved and that salvation has been won for us. Finally, he wants our faith in him to affect our lives. He wants us to change our ways so that we witness to him and live joyfully the good news he has come to preach.

We are truly blessed if we have faith. Jesus told Thomas: "Happy are those who have not seen and yet believe" (Jn 20:29). The Letter to the Hebrews gives us a beautiful definition of faith: "Faith is confident assurance concerning what we hope for, and conviction about things we do not see" (Heb 11:1, *New American Bible*).

Faith in Jesus is a lifelong task. It need not knock us off a horse as it did St. Paul. It can be a more subtle growth where we approach Jesus with increasing confidence, inviting him more and more to influence and take over our lives.

Jesus invites us to accept him and to respond to him. Lived faith is our response. Faith is a kind of vision. We need it to see Jesus. We need it to walk confidently with him. We need it to see clearly what is really important in life.

Christians have used the following ways to find Jesus in the world. They help us to see him and give us the strength to respond to him. You should find all of them extremely helpful in growing in the spiritual life.

CHRIST IS PRESENT IN HIS CHURCH

We belong to Jesus Christ by virtue of membership in the Catholic church. The church is the body of Christ. Jesus is its head and we are its members.

Vatican II teaches how Jesus is active in the world today through the church:

Christ, having been lifted up from the earth, is drawing all men to Himself (Jn. 12:32, Greek text). Rising from the dead (cf. Rom. 6:9), He sent His life-giving Spirit upon His disciples and through this Spirit has established His body, the Church, as the universal sacrament of salvation. Sitting at the right hand of the Father, He is continually active in the world, leading men to the Church, and through her joining them more closely to Himself and making them partakers of His glorious life by nourishing them with His own body and blood (*Dogmatic Constitution on the Church,* No. 48).

The power of the Holy Spirit unites us into the body of the Lord to continue his work of salvation and sanctification. The *Body of Christ* is a powerful image. It means every member has a role to play in continuing Jesus' work.

By baptism we become members of Jesus' body. In a sense we are the hands of Jesus in the world today continuing his healing touch. We possess the power of his understanding glance which looks out on the world with love. Similarly, on Jesus' behalf, we speak words of forgiveness. The Holy Spirit empowers us to live a Christlike life.

You and your Christian brothers and sisters—the church of Jesus Christ—are Jesus Christ present in the world today. Look to yourself as a special presence of Jesus in the world. Look to your Christian brothers and sisters as Christ present in the world today.

BODY OF CHRIST

1. Share with a friend a time when you felt that you were Jesus Christ for another person.

   Alternative: Write a short essay addressing this question.

2. Because Jesus lives in our fellow Christians by the power of the Holy Spirit, we ought to treasure and deeply respect each other. Examine how well you cherish your Christian brothers

and sisters by responding to the following items. Mark according to this scale.

3 — this describes me pretty well

2 — this describes me most of the time

1 — I need to work on this

____ I respect my fellow believers.

____ I usually see good in others even if I don't agree with everything they do or say.

____ I appreciate that others have gifts that I don't have.

____ I believe that our Lord works through others.

3. If the Lord lives in you, then you have been gifted by the Spirit to do his work. In his Letter to the Galatians (5:22), St. Paul lists the so-called *fruits of the Holy Spirit* which are concrete evidence that a person is cooperating with the indwelling of the Lord.

Check one of the following which, in your estimation, demonstrates that you are very much a part of the vine of Christ.

____ *love*: I am giving and compassionate. I see others with the eyes of Jesus.

____ *joy*: I am creatively alive, even in the midst of trials, because of my deep faith in God's love.

____ *peace*: I experience a personal harmony that flows from a deep conviction of acceptance by the Lord.

____ *patience*: I am able to accept my own and other people's limitations.

____ *kindness*: I respond to the needs of others. I am caring and empathetic.

____ *goodness*: I am honest, wholesome, guileless.

____ *trustfulness*: I am faithful even under the severest trials.

____ *gentleness*: I am humble. I show appreciation for others and for the gifts I've been given.

____ *self-control*: I am disciplined. I can say no to myself.

JESUS AND THE SACRAMENTS

Vatican II reminds us of the many ways Jesus is present to the Christian community, especially in its worship. Reflect on the following passage:

> Christ is always present in His Church, especially in her liturgical celebrations. He is present in the sacrifice of the Mass, not only in the person of His minister, "the same one now offering, through the ministry of priests, who formerly offered himself on the cross," but especially under the Eucharistic species. By His power He is present in the sacraments, so that when a man baptizes it is really Christ Himself who baptizes. He is present in His word, since it is He Himself who speaks when the holy Scriptures are read in the church. He is present, finally, when the Church prays and sings, for He promised: "Where two or three are gathered together for my sake, there am I in the midst of them" (*Constitution on the Sacred Liturgy*, No. 7).

This passage includes some key Catholic beliefs about how Jesus is present to us and how we can meet him. We will comment on several of the points made.

First, Jesus is present in the sacraments. The sacraments are moments of encounter with the living Lord. They are external signs which bring about an interior grace. They are tangible ways in which the Lord touches us in Christian community, meaningful encounters for us humans who need concrete reminders of God's abiding presence.

In **baptism,** for example, our Lord extends to us the invitation and privilege to join his body, the church. Through the presence and concern of other Christians, he promises to support us on our life's journey to the Father. **Confirmation** strengthens our faith commitment by showering on us the gifts of the Spirit. In the sacrament of **matrimony** the Lord joins a couple as they venture on the exciting but difficult vocation. He promises to be with them in their lovemaking, in their daily struggles to be faithful, in the trials and tribulations that inevitably come. In **holy orders** the Lord is present to the Christian community through special ministers who have been appointed to serve the church and lead it in worship. In the sacrament of **the anointing of the sick** Jesus sustains us spiritually and sometimes heals us physically. He meets us in many of the key events of our life—at birth, in sickness, when we need adult strength to live out his mandate to love others, when we choose a state in life.

We also appreciate meeting Jesus in two sacraments that are available to us as often as we choose to celebrate them—the sacraments of reconciliation and the Eucharist.

Reconciliation is a great way to meet Jesus and receive his healing touch of forgiveness. Today's emphasis in the sacrament is on reconciliation with the Christian community. When we sin we have harmed our relationship with God and with others. From time to time, especially when we have sinned seriously, we need to ask for God's pardon, express our sorrow, experience the reassurance of our Lord's forgiveness and heal any wounds we have caused in Christ's body. Many Catholics find a caring, loving, sensitive Jesus in this sacrament, a Jesus who accepts them in their weakness and gives them the strength to try again to live the great vocation of love that he has bestowed on them.

The passage quoted on page 210 informs us of various presences of the Lord, many of them coming together in the **Eucharist.** We Catholics believe that Jesus is truly present, body and blood, in the bread and wine consecrated in the eucharistic liturgy (the Mass). We believe that when we receive holy communion, we receive the Lord himself. We further believe that the Eucharist is our greatest source of strength and nourishment as Christians. We receive the Lord to be transformed by him, that is, to allow him to live through us as we meet and serve people in our daily life. The concluding words of the Mass, "Go, you are sent," remind us that we receive Jesus not to keep him to ourselves but to let him shine through us as we become "light of the world" and "salt of the earth."

Jesus is also present in the eucharistic celebration in the priest who leads us in worship. He is present in our brothers and sisters who come to celebrate what Jesus has done for us. He is present, in addition, in the reading of the word which reminds us of the great deeds God has accomplished for us.

Scripture reading is a powerful word of God. When the Bible is read quietly and reflectively, it can and does change lives. As the great Protestant missionary to Africa, David Livingstone, said: "All that I am I owe to Jesus Christ revealed to me in his divine book."

We meet Jesus in the Eucharist—in the celebrant, in our fellow Christians gathered in his name, in the reading of the word, in his body and blood. The Eucharist is the summit of Christian worship. It both celebrates and creates Christian community. It is a peak moment in our Christian lives, a moment when we share and celebrate the Lord together. We unite ourselves to the Lord to allow him to work through us in our love and service of others. If we approach the Eucharist with true faith, then we will be changed and so will those who meet us in our everyday lives.

REFLECTIONS

1. As a class, list some reasons why people don't go to Mass. Some examples are provided. Then respond to the reason or offer a solution to the problem the person is having.

   Reason: I can worship God better by myself.
   Response: Jesus asked us to gather together in his name. We need each other on our journey to our Father.

   Reason: It's boring.

   Response: _____

   Reason: All they do is ask for money.

   Response: _____

   Reason: I don't like being with a bunch of phonies.

   Response: _____

   Reason: _____

   Response: _____

   Reason: _____

   Response: _____

   Reason: _____

   Response: _____

2. *Try this*:
   a. Find a restful place. Relax. Put yourself in the presence of the Lord.
   b. Pick a gospel passage where Jesus speaks. Put yourself in the setting of this passage.
   c. Slowly and meditatively read this passage, imagining that Jesus is speaking to you. Reflect on the meaning of the words. Ask the Lord to help you see what the passage might mean for you.
   d. After the reading, spend a few moments of quiet,

reflective time with the Lord. Thank him for being present to you. Thank him for the great gifts he has given you. Ask him to help you live the message of the scripture passage you have read.

e. *Optional*: Jot down your impressions in a prayer diary and come back to them at a later date.

MEETING JESUS IN PRAYER

To know and to experience Jesus as a personal friend demand that we spend time with him. All friendships are built on communication and availability. Friends are open to each other and make a sincere attempt to get to know each other. Prayer is an excellent way to develop our friendship with Jesus Christ.

Prayer is talking with God, spending time with him, becoming aware of him, allowing him to contact us and come into our lives.

We saw how reading scripture can be a prayerful encounter with the living Lord. But simply putting ourselves in the presence of the Lord—talking to him in our own words or relaxing in his presence and saying nothing at all—is also a way to reach out to the Lord who is always there caring for us.

Reading prayers composed by others or books on spirituality can help the Christian who wants to pray. Reciting traditional formula prayers (like the Our Father) slowly and meaningfully helps many people contact the living God. Reflecting on how God works through the people and events that come into our lives can also be prayerful.

Prayer should always be humble and sincere. Jesus taught us to pray the Our Father, the model prayer. He taught us to approach God as Abba, and to praise God for all he has created. He taught us to pray for the advent of God's kingdom and that his will be done. In prayer, Christians try to discover what God wants for them. Jesus instructed us to ask for our daily bread; our deep concerns are God's deep concerns. Our Lord told us to ask for forgiveness and reminded us that we too must extend forgiveness. Finally Jesus told us to pray that we not be put to the test and that we be delivered from evil.

We can pray anytime and anywhere. But it is a good idea to have a special time and a special place for conversing with the Lord.

Prayer can be tough. Distractions will inevitably come our way. But merely attempting to pray, trying to meet the Lord, is itself a prayer. No one who prays is left unchanged. The Lord will meet you if you want him to. That someone "out there" will become a personal, vital friend who will change you. He will enable you to love others as he loves you. It is worth the effort.

JESUS ON PRAYER

Here are some of Jesus' most famous words on prayer. Reflect on them carefully. Judge your own faith response to them.

1 — I firmly believe this

2 — I want to believe this

3 — I'm not sure this is true

_____ 1. "In your prayers do not babble as the pagans do, for they think that by using many words they will make themselves heard" (Mt 6:7).

_____ 2. "So I say to you: Ask, and it will be given to you; search, and you will find; knock, and the door will be opened to you" (Lk 11:9).

_____ 3. "For everyone who exalts himself will be humbled, but the man who humbles himself will be exalted" (Lk 18:14).

Discussion: Share with your classmates a time when you felt drawn to the Lord through prayer. When has prayer helped you?

FINDING CHRIST IN OTHERS

Jesus continually challenges us to find him in other people. In fact, the message of the parable of the Good Samaritan is that everyone, even our enemy, is our neighbor and worthy of our respect and love. Jesus asks us how can we love the God whom we cannot see if we cannot love the neighbor whom we can see. The proof of our love of the Lord is the love of our neighbor.

Jesus strongly identified himself with the lowly, the outcast, those who were not accepted by the well-established. He taught that we will be judged by how we welcome the stranger, feed the hungry, give drink to the thirsty, visit the sick and the imprisoned.

> "I tell you solemnly, in so far as you neglected to
> do this to one of the least of these, you neglected
> to do it to me" (Mt 25:45).

We must find Jesus in others. Active love for others is the measure of our faith and our commitment as his disciples. We need not look far. Those who are closest to us need our love—family, friends, classmates. The lonely, the misunderstood and the mistreated all need us to pay attention to them. The poor, the handicapped, the retarded, the aged are waiting for our care. Victims of prejudice are all around us. Our Lord wants us to see him in all these people and to go out of our way to love them, to meet their needs, to give them our friendship.

The Christian community has many models of holiness past and present. The saints are people who have cultivated a deep friendship with the Lord, a friendship so strong that it is easy to see Christ through their lives. They show us what it means to respond to the "least of these."

Mary, the Mother of God, is the supreme symbol of Christian holiness. Her entire life is a model to us all. Mary let her life become the words she spoke to the angel Gabriel: "I am the handmaid of the Lord, let what you have said be done to me" (Lk 1:38). These humble words of openness to God are what we all pray for when we pray "Thy will be done" in the Our Father. By allowing God's will to be done, Mary brought Christ into the world. By allowing God's will to be done, we do the same.

The life of each saint sheds a unique perspective on how Jesus comes into the world through a heroic Christian. St. Paul, for example, was a man of fire and passion, a man of deep conviction who risked all to spread the good news of Jesus. His life reminds us that we can't be lukewarm in our Christian commitment. Francis of Assisi demonstrates that to be Christlike means to have a deep compassion for the poor. St. Therese of Lisieux shows us that a simple life of prayer and doing ordinary things in an extraordinary manner is a way to find Christ. St. Thomas More tells us that Christ and his church must be number one in our life; allegiance to another—even a king—cannot be above our allegiance to God.

In our own day there are countless men and women who reveal through their actions that they see Jesus in others. Mother Teresa, a woman committed to serving the most destitute of people, does so for precisely this reason. She loves everyone because she sees Jesus in everyone.

People close to you may well be unsung heroes whose lives are worth imitating. Can you see Christ in the love of your mother and father, in their care and concern for you? Can you see Jesus teaching you through your instructors, training your mind so that you can one day help others more effectively? Do you see the Lord in the person who rides on the same bus with you? Do you see the face of Jesus in everyone who comes into your life? He is there. We need but look.

The Christian never forgets that he or she is also Christ. The Lord has chosen each of us to be his ambassador, his missionary of love. He comes into the world through us. His love touches others if we love.

TWO PROJECTS

Research the life of a favorite Christian saint or contemporary person committed to seeing Jesus in others. Prepare a report that discusses how this person sees Christ in others and how you see Christ in this person's life.

As an alternative to the above, interview the most Christlike person you know. Ask where he or she finds Jesus in the world today. Also ask about the role of the sacraments (especially the Eucharist), prayer and Bible reading in his or her life. Report your findings to the class.

SUMMARY

1. Jesus wants his followers to have faith in him, a lived faith that enables us to see his active presence in the world and empowers us to respond to his command to love.

2. The Lord is active in the world today through his body, the church. By the power of the Holy Spirit he is present through Christians who cooperate with his continuing work of salvation.

3. Christians experience the presence of Jesus in a special way when they worship. The Lord is present at the eucharistic liturgy under the form of bread and wine, in the celebrant, in the worshiping community and in the reading of the word. In addition, the Lord encounters the Christian in baptism and confirmation, in the sacraments of reconciliation and the anointing of the sick and in the sacraments of vocation—matrimony and holy orders.

4. Prayer is an essential way to contact and develop a friendship with the living Lord. Prayer should be simple, sincere and humble.

5. Christ lives in others. He taught us that whenever we respond to others, especially the outcast, we respond to him. To be a disciple of Jesus means we must love everyone. The saints provide a powerful example of what it means to love. Christ shines through their lives. Mary, the mother of God, is the preeminent example of Christian faith, of a person open to God's will. Her life is especially worthy of imitation.

PRAYER EXERCISE

All good Christian art that deals with Mary and Jesus depicts Mary in such a way that she draws attention not to herself but to Jesus. For example, consider the famous statue of Mary holding her dead son in her arms, *The Pieta.* There our attention is drawn to Jesus.

All good Marian devotions also lead us to Christ. Perhaps the most popular Marian devotion in the Catholic church is the rosary. It combines traditional vocal prayers with meditation on key mysteries of our faith. These mysteries revolve around the important events which have won our salvation.

Now that you are near the end of your study about Jesus, you should find it very valuable as a class to recite the 15 decades of the rosary together (perhaps spread out over three days). Meditate on the great things God has done for you through his son Jesus.

The Joyful Mysteries

1. The Annunciation
2. The Visitation of Mary to Elizabeth
3. The Birth of Jesus
4. The Presentation of Jesus in the Temple
5. The Finding of Jesus in the Temple

The Sorrowful Mysteries

1. The Agony of Jesus in the Garden
2. The Scourging at the Pillar
3. The Crowning With Thorns
4. The Carrying of the Cross
5. The Crucifixion

The Glorious Mysteries

1. The Resurrection of Jesus
2. The Ascension of Jesus into Heaven
3. The Descent of the Holy Spirit Upon the Apostles
4. The Assumption of Mary Into Heaven
5. The Crowning of Mary As Queen of Heaven

Conclusion

"All who call on the name of the Lord will be saved."
—Acts 2:21

We have discussed the Jesus of history and have seen the special role of the gospels. We have looked at the world in which Jesus lived and taught, examined his personality, and observed how each gospel writer presents him. We have studied the message of Jesus and reflected on the central role of the paschal mystery in our salvation. We have seen what the early church and Christians through the centuries have believed about Jesus and how Christians today picture him. Finally, we have reflected on how we today can contact the living Lord.

And after all this Jesus still asks you: "Who do you say that I am?" Is he your personal friend? Is he God's Son, a savior who has redeemed you from sin and death? Is he your guide and model for living a life of service to others? Is he the Lord of the universe? Is he the answer to your most profound questions? Or is Jesus still a question mark?

This book may have served to help you know more *about* Jesus, thus aiding you in your journey of faith. But you may still be searching for an answer to Jesus' question, "Who do you say that I am?" There is still so much more to know about Jesus. St. John realized this when he ended his gospel this way:

> There were many other things that Jesus did; if all were written down, the world itself, I suppose, would not hold all the books that would have to be written (Jn 21:25).

We need to continue our study of Jesus and read more about him. But we also realize that reading a book or even many books about Jesus is not enough. Our real task is to *know* Jesus.

For Christians, knowing Jesus as a friend is the most important thing in life. We believe he is the source of true happiness. But to know Jesus requires something of us:

- First and foremost, we must accept Jesus as the living Lord and as a personal friend. We must never forget that God loves us beyond human imagination. There is nothing we can do that he won't forgive. Jesus came for each one of us. He loves us all. He wants to be our friend.

- We must spend time in personal prayer getting to know him.

- We need to break bread regularly with our fellow Christians.

- We must ask for forgiveness when we sin and try to right the wrongs we have done.

- We need to make a serious attempt to model our life on the life of Jesus, to serve others in some way and show special concern for the "least" of our brothers and sisters.

A PRAYER FOR STUDENTS

May the Lord be with you on your journey!
May he be ever ready to lighten your burdens.
May he give you the ability to see him more clearly,
   love him more dearly,
   and follow him more nearly
every day of your life.

A JESUS CATECHISM

Here are some questions you should be able to answer about Jesus now that you have finished this book. If you are able to discuss these intelligently, you have grasped many of the major ideas you have studied.

1. What does the name *Jesus* mean and why is it appropriate that our Lord was given this name?

2. What can the Christian say in response to the charge that there was no historical Jesus?

3. Discuss how the gospels came to be, and tell something about each of them.

4. Explain the importance and significance of Jesus' use of *Abba, Amen,* his parables and his teaching on love.

5. Discuss some of major events of the history of the Jews, and how these events may have contributed to the expectation of a messiah in Jesus' day.

6. Identify and briefly comment on the significance of Herod the Great, Pontius Pilate, Herod Antipas, the Pharisees, the Sadducees, the Essenes and the Zealots.

7. What was everyday life like in our Lord's day? Discuss several aspects.

8. What might Jesus have looked like? Justify your description.

9. What was the human Jesus like? You may wish to comment on some of the following traits: his sensitivity; his friendship with others; his teaching ability; his genuineness.

10. What did Jesus teach? Can his message still mean something to people today? Explain. Is it meaningful to you? Explain.

11. Each of the gospel writers has his own unique portrait of Jesus. Briefly discuss how two of the gospels present Jesus. Use several examples from each to substantiate your discussion.

12. What is the meaning of the death of Jesus?

13. Why is the resurrection absolutely essential to our salvation and to our faith in Jesus?

14. What are some objections people have raised of the resurrection? How might we respond?

15. How can Christians live the paschal mystery in their daily lives?

16. Discuss the meaning and significance of each of the following New Testament titles of Jesus:
    a. Christ
    b. Suffering Servant
    c. Lord
    d. Son of Man
    e. Son of God
    f. Word of God
    g. Prophet, Priest, King

17. How does Jesus continue to teach today?

18. Discuss two early heresies concerning Jesus. How did the church respond to these heresies?

19. Discuss several key doctrines about Jesus which have come down to us from the early councils. Be sure to mention the teaching of the Council of Chalcedon (451) and discuss its meaning.

20. Discuss one contemporary theological question about Jesus.

21. What is your favorite image of Jesus? Discuss it and describe why it is particularly meaningful to you.

22. What are some helpful images of Jesus derived from the media? What are some harmful ones? Discuss why these either add to or subtract from a good understanding of Jesus.

23. What is faith?

24. Discuss how Jesus is present in his church, in the sacraments and in scripture reading.

25. Where can you personally encounter Jesus today? What does he expect of his friends?

BIBLE SERVICE

A bible service is a form of shared prayer which focuses on reading and reflecting on God's word.

Many themes can serve to unify a scripture service, for example, forgiveness, concern for others, friendship in the Lord, giftedness, unity, faith, life in Christ.

A good setting is essential for a prayerful bible service. Comfortable seats, candles, burning incense, flowers, and banners which display the theme all contribute to a prayerful atmosphere.

As a class, celebrate Jesus in a bible service. Begin by selecting a theme which the class feels highlights an outstanding trait of Jesus. You might check a concordance to the bible which lists all the references of a particular word used in the bible or one of the many excellent dictionaries of the bible to select readings for your service. Arrange for volunteers to prepare the music, banners, etc.

Here is a suggested plan:

> Opening Hymn
> First Reading
> > *Silent reflection*
> Second Reading
> > *Silent reflection*
> Third Reading
> Homily
> > *Spontaneous prayer*
> The Our Father
> Concluding Prayer
> Closing Hymn